Design After Modernism

FURNITURE AND INTERIORS 1970 ~ 2010

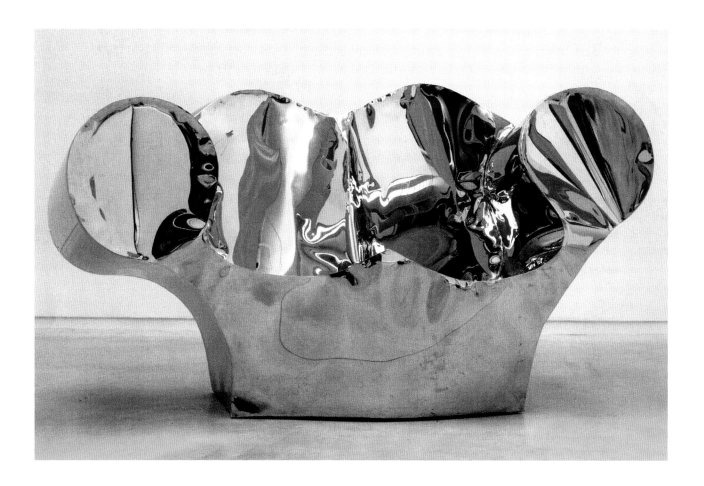

PREVIOUS PAGE

Satan's Tongue, Michael Coffey (United States)
ca. 1989
Burled wood, plate glass

This is one of several versions named for its provocative form. Each was slightly different, of varying carved
and laminated exotic woods. Coffey's woodworking,
which began as a hobby, is closer to art furniture than
to studio craft in its expressiveness and unconventional forms. In East Coast studios in four states, he
has produced his unique designs for more than three
decades, during which he founded two crafts schools
and woodworking training programs.

ABOVE

Big Easy Volume 2 for 2, Ron Arad
(United Kingdom, b. Israel)
1989
Polished stainless steel

Combining machine technology and one-off fabrication, the parts of this design are mechanically cut
from a pattern, but seams are welded by hand,
creating varying effects. Since the sides are uneven,
the polished surface distorts reflections. The material
suggests rigidity, while the form implies comfort.
This is a unique piece; others were made in black, and
a one-seat version was made in injection-molded foam.

Design After Modernism

FURNITURE AND INTERIORS 1970 ~ 2010

JUDITH GURA

Original Renderings by Sophia Yi-Ying Lu

W. W. NORTON & COMPANY | NEW YORK LONDON

Blushing Zettel'z, Ingo Maurer
(Germany)
1997/2005
Japanese paper, stainless steel,
heat-resistant satin-frosted glass
An interactive chandelier, with
sheets of clipped-on paper in place
of the expected crystal drops, this
limited-edition variation has 80 sheets
of elegant erotic images; another has
love letters (some blank); and still

another scribbled drawings. The sheets
can be rearranged or replaced with the
user's own images. It was also made
with blank sheets. Maurer is known
for his highly original lighting, most
intended for serial production. He has
also designed public light installations
and developed many applications for
LEDs and organic LEDs (light-emitting
diodes).

For information about permission to reproduce selections from this
book, write to Permissions, W. W. Norton & Company, Inc., 500
Fifth Avenue, New York, NY 10110

For information about special discounts for bulk purchases, please
contact W. W. Norton Special Sales at specialsales@wwnorton.com
or 800-233-4830

Manufacturing by KHL Printing
Book design by Guenet Abraham
Production manager: Leeann Graham

Library of Congress Cataloging-in-Publication Data

Gura, Judith.

Design after modernism : furniture and interiors, 1970-2010 / Judith
Gura ; original renderings by Sophia Yi-Ying Lu. — 1st ed.
     p. cm.
 Includes bibliographical references and index.
 ISBN 978-0-393-73304-4 (hardcover)

1. Design—History—20th century. 2. Modernism (Aesthetics) I.
Lu, Sophia Yi-Ying. II. Title.
 NK1390.G87 2012
 749.09'04—dc23
2011028210

ISBN: 978-0-393-73304-4
W. W. Norton & Company, Inc.
500 Fifth Avenue, New York, N.Y. 10110

www.wwnorton.com

W. W. Norton & Company Ltd.
Castle House, 75/76 Wells Street
London W1T 3QT

0 9 8 7 6 5 4 3 2 1

To Mason, who has also been published

Nara Chair, Shin Azumi (Japan)
2010
Wood, leather or fabric upholstery

Sleek interpretation of a chair, reminiscent of Asian foam.

Rainbow Chair, Patrick Norguet (France)
2000
Acrylic resin

Modern material meets old-fashioned optimism in a colorful design suggesting a celebration of good things ahead. The different-color segments are joined by ultrasound. Norguet was named Designer of the Year in 2005 by *Wallpaper* magazine.

Smoke Dining Armchair, Maarten Baas (Netherlands)
2009
Epoxy-finished burnt wood, fire retardant foam, leather upholstery

Conceptual design that's more than meets the eye ... a discarded chair was radically transformed by human intervention, burned with a blowtorch to create an intense black surface which was then coated with resin and lacquer. No two in the series are exactly alike ... yet each retain the outline of its original form. One of these was included in European Design Since 1985.

CONTENTS

V.I.P. Chair, Marcel Wanders
(Netherlands)
2000
Felt upholstery, steel

Chunky and assertive, this chair sits
importantly on tapered squat legs, with
meticulously finished seams that suggest
a custom-tailored overcoat. It appeared
in the exhibition European Design Since
1985: Shaping the New Century.

Neve Chair, Piero Lissoni (Italy)
2010
Stained ash in black, natural,
red or mongoi

A modern take on a classic form, but
shaped in varying thicknesses of wood.

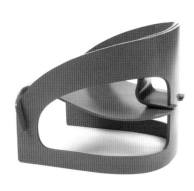

Armchair with Curved Elements
Joe Colombo (Italy)
1964
Lacquered wood

Assembled like a jigsaw puzzle
from three bent and molded pieces
of plywood, this design prefigured
Colombo's later work in plastics.
Introduced at the Salone del
Mobile in 1965, it has starred in
several major museum exhibitions,
including Italy: The New Domestic
Landscape, Design Since 1945, and
Design 1935-1965: What Modern
Was. Colombo, one of the most tal-
ented and prolific of the midcentury
Italian designers, died at the young
age of forty-one.

Counterpoint Occasional Table
Michael Coffey (United States)
1984
Laminated and carved Mozambique
wood

Ceiling Light, Max Sauze (France)
c. 1960s
Aluminum

Pelikan Armchair, Finn Juhl (Denmark)
1940 reintroduced 2008
Steel frame, plastic/MDI, walnut, canvas/linen,
foam and fiber, hand-sewn upholstery

An early work by a legendary Danish designer,
an anthropomorphic form is revived for contemporary Modernism's inclusive vocabulary.

VarioPillo Sectional Seating
Burkhard Vogtherr (Germany)
1970
Upholstery, plastic

A variation of the endlessly extendable
modular sofas pioneered by Italian designers in
the post-World War II decades.

Crinoline Chair with High Backrest
Patricia Urquiola (Spain)
2008
Weather-resistant painted aluminum frame,
bronze rope and natural rope interlacing,
cushion

Named for the stiff undergarment fabric it
recalls, this cocoon-shape high-back chair, made
by Philippine artisans, is deceptively fragile in
appearance but designed to withstand the elements in outdoor use. Urquiola, one of relatively
few prominent women furniture designers, now
works in Italy. Her designs are in the collection
of the Museum of Modern Art, among others.

PREFACE

Paradise Tree Coat Rack, Oiva Toikka
(Finland)
2009
Polyethylene, galvanized steel

Most books about Modern design end the story at the mid-twentieth century. It is time for an update.

The word itself is problematical; although it dates to medieval times, when "modern" referred to current or recent events, it became an aesthetic term only in the eighteenth century. Since then, design historians, practitioners, and critics have been debating about its meaning and devising labels for its many incarnations. The twentieth century brought a new challenge: a succession of sometimes-overlapping styles ending in a coda of pluralism that may be among the century's most memorable legacies. This diversity nurtured opposing schools of designers—those who sought to merge tradition with progressive ideas, and those who abandoned precedent in pursuit of the avant-garde. The former created works that honored history; the latter conceived archetypes of particular moments in time. Both are integral to the history of Modernism and must be incorporated into its vocabulary. Provoking more heated debate over the past few decades, the diversification of forms, materials, and technologies confused the issue, defying efforts to place design objects into categories.

In contemporary parlance, Modernism generally refers to the aesthetic that evolved from the Bauhaus and flourished at midcentury, disseminating worldwide into variants of what became the International Style. Though it professed to abandon the very notion of style, International Style architecture became as formulaic as most of its predecessors, and so did its interiors. Modern furnishings adopted a fixed set of characteristics: silhouettes were spare and machine-fabricated; ornament was eschewed; and references to historicism were studiously avoided.

Those guidelines are no longer relevant. The Modernism of midcentury has receded into history, and today's inclusive, transformed, and reenergized version embraces a cornucopia of design in an almost-endless range of materials. Like its earlier manifestations, today's Modernism accepts industrialization and values functionalism, but, unlike them, it employs tools and technologies never before possible, allows the option of decoration, and may incorporate elements drawn from the past. These changes are accompanied by an expanded design profession; interiors and furniture are being created by architects, interior designers, furniture makers, industrial designers, artisans, artists—even fashion designers—some of whom cross disciplines to work in several areas. The result of these and

other factors has been to broaden the scope of design, blurring the boundaries between designer and artist and between the manufactured and the handmade.

This book gives an overview of the developments in Modern design over the past four decades—some evolutionary, some expected, and some extraordinary. It identifies the varied and sometimes overlapping directions, approaches, and movements that have challenged the orthodoxy of Modernism. Each of these directions has generated designs that reflect the contexts in which they were created; and some of the most

Lampros 3, Ceiling Lamp
Ettore Sottsass (Italy, b. Austria)
1975
Enameled steel, enameled and polished aluminum, glass

Best known for more radical works, Sottsass designed industrial objects for Olivetti from 1959, including the bright-red Valentine typewriter (1969). A leader of Italy's 1970s Radical Design movement, he would later become the face of Postmodernism, founding the Memphis design collaborative and designing some of its most familiar works.

Miss Dorn Chair, Philippe Starck
(France)
1982
Metal, leather upholstery

This chair is more abstract than most of Starck's designs, though following his penchant for witty names. Starck is a versatile designer of interiors and products, whose designs for accessories and mass-produced household items like juicers and toothbrushes have been as widely published as his attention-getting hotel and restaurant interiors.

characteristic, most noteworthy, and most innovative of them are illustrated, along with renderings of archetypical interiors that suggest the types of environments they furnished.

The objects shown in the pages that follow were chosen as much for their imaginative form, sophisticated technology, effective use of materials, and originality of concept as for visual appeal. In another era, some would not have been considered significant, memorable, or attractive—nor, to some, may they be so now. They are, however, indisputably representative of their time. Whether they will be admired in times to come remains to be seen.

Bubbles Chaise, Frank Gehry
(United States, b. Canada)
1987
Cardboard

A later variation on Gehry's series of
furniture designs made from corrugated
cardboard. Part of the Experimental
Edges series, this piece is in the collection
of the Museum of Modern Art.

Chair One, Konstantin Grcic
(Germany)
2003
Polished or anodized aluminum, with
die-cast aluminum treated with sput-
tered fluorinated titanium, polyester
powder paint

Jagged lines converge in a stacking chair
designed to cradle the body. Grcic, who
originally trained as a cabinetmaker,
has received international awards for
his striking minimalist designs, which
have included household objects and
exhibitions as well as furniture.

Concrete Jungle, Jonas Bohlin
(Sweden)
2007
Lacquered steel, concrete, handmade
candles, aquarium gravel

ACKNOWLEDGMENTS

Although my name is most prominent, this book owes its publication to the helping hands of others without whom it would have remained merely an outline:

Nancy Green and Nancy Palmquist at W. W. Norton, whose encouragement and guidance saw me through the effort to make sense of a time period that is still too recent to judge objectively. Libby Burton, for juggling documents and details with good-natured calm;

Guenet Abraham, for her artistry in designing a beautiful book to frame my words and show off the images;

Sophia Lu, who rose to the challenge of illustrating rooms that typified the various time periods and style directions of recent Modernism. Her creative skills and her deft use of computer rendering bring the interiors I describe to life;

The New York School of Interior Design and its president, Christopher Cyphers, for continuing professional support of my activities, in and outside of school;

Lara Huchteman, whose organizational skills with image-collection, spreadsheets and follow-up enabled me to focus on research and writing;

The auction houses (with special thanks to Alex Payne, David Rago, and Richard Wright) dealers, producers and designers who generously supplied the images that accompany my words and put into pictures the forms, materials, techniques, and exceptional variety of recent modern design; and Martin Gura, trusted sounding board, first reader, critic, and cheering section.

Crochet Chair, Marcel Wanders
(Netherlands)
2006
Crocheted fiber and epoxy resin

Modern technology transforms a
grandmotherly craft: individual, hand-
crocheted flowers are stitched together,
formed on a mold, and stiffened with
resin. Made as a limited edition of
twenty for Art Basel Miami Beach 2006.

S Chair, Verner Panton (Denmark)
1960
Injection-molded polypropylene

The first one-piece injection-molded
plastic chair—whose cantilevered form
was a concept ahead of its time. Technical problems in fabrication (it had to
be both sturdy and stackable) delayed
production until seven years after it was
designed. Panton had made a laminated

version in 1955. Featured in Design
1935-1965: What Modern Was and
most every major museum collection,
it was the most advanced design in
plastic made outside of Italy in the
midcentury years.

INTRODUCTION

Modernism's first revolution came as the twentieth century began. It coalesced in the midcentury decades, establishing design parameters that defined a generation. A century later, another revolution is under way—one in which science and technology may transform design, and our environment, even more radically than the first. To understand these changes, it is necessary to reexamine the convoluted history of the style (or styles) we call Modernism.

PROGRESSIONS
OF A STYLE

The first stirrings of what we think of as Modernism arose in the wake of the Industrial Revolution, when the machinery for mass production unleashed a profusion of poorly conceived designs on an unsophisticated and unsuspecting public. Critics of the Great Exhibition of 1851, in London's Crystal Palace, bemoaned the tastelessly overdecorated objects and mourned

the marginalization of the craftsman. Inspired by the polemics of writer and critic John Ruskin, designers of the Arts & Crafts movement revived handcraftsmanship but unrealistically rejected the machine. Art Nouveau took another path, drawing inspiration from nature rather than history in its search for a new aesthetic. As the twentieth century got under way, the movement toward a Modernism that rejected the past outright coexisted with the lingering heritage of historicism—but in uneasy equilibrium. Not until 1918, when Walter Gropius established the school and workshops of the Bauhaus, was an

Scandia Lounge Chair, Hans Brattrud
(Norway)
1957
Lacquered wood, steel
Norway's most celebrated contribution to midcentury Scandinavian design.

Orange Slice Chairs, Pierre Paulin
(France)
1960
Beech, upholstery, tubular steel
Curvy forms like these and other Paulin seating designs, descended from the Museum of Modern Art's Organic Design exhibition of 1949, helped move biomorphism into the mainstream. These chairs became icons of midcentury design, along with those of the Eameses and Eero Saarinen.

attempt made to reconcile man and machine, giving equal status to fine and decorative arts and designing objects specifically for industrial production.

As critical discourse converged into a broader acceptance of Modernism, new standards were codified for all its applications: form must follow function (i.e., practicality

trumped aesthetics), silhouettes were restrained, new materials and technology were embraced, and decoration was deemed unsuitable. In architecture, defined primarily by the International Style, structural balance supplanted classical symmetry and applied ornament was scrupulously avoided. This was a style made possible by the availability of modern materials and new construction methods: with walls freed of their load-bearing role, interiors could be contiguous volumes, uninterrupted by ceiling-high divisions. Though curvilinear forms

Tete-a-Tete, Edward Wormley
(United States)
1960
Upholstery, walnut, brass
Update of a Victorian-era form,
by a modernist who refused to
reject historicism.

were not entirely abandoned (see Le Corbusier's Villa Savoye), rectilinearity was the preferred geometry. Unfortunately, however, adherence to a strict set of principles and the demotion of aesthetic concerns (to the detriment of the latter) led to architecture that was uncomfortably homogeneous.

Meanwhile, interior and furniture designers pursued their respective efforts to recast the world in modern form, embracing the machine and mass production while accepting the limitations these imposed. After Frank Lloyd Wright and Mies van der Rohe, the modern residence had become a continuum of interrelated spaces. Surfaces that would previously have been carved, paneled, or plastered were smooth and unbroken, and expanses of windows spanned the divide between exterior and interior. The principle of integrating the house into the landscape, or the building into its context, was taken for granted—though not invariably observed. (Such changes, of course, were rarely possible to implement in apartment and townhouse residences, which developed their own variations on the Modernist vocabulary.) Echoing the architectural aesthetic, furniture reflected a concern with function in spare but shapely silhouettes, natural materials and finishes, and the virtual eradication of decorative motifs.

The Second World War, with its cataclysmic effects on both political power and social circumstances, marked the great divide in twentieth-century design—for better and, occasionally, for worse. The following decades saw the emergence of several centers of style and many, often competing, arbiters of taste. With peacetime came a period of optimism and prosperity, and the resulting wave of postwar construction acquainted the public with the architecture of High Modernism. New buildings by Mies van der Rohe and his contemporaries were lauded as fine art, conveying status on their occupants as well as their creators. Although the ethos of "Good Design," as presented in the Museum of Modern Art's influential 1950–55 exhibitions, proselytized a new aesthetic for all to enjoy, the disciplined ambience of Modernism was, for some time, the exclusive province of the intellectual elite. Their fashion-

Three-Arm Floor Lamp, Arredoluce
(Italy)
1960
Enameled and chrome-plated steel, enameled aluminum, marble, leather, chrome-plated brass
Probably the most familiar, and most copied, icon of Italy's modern lighting designs.

Hand Chairs, Pedro Friedeberg
(Mexico)
1971
Lacquered wood
Entirely unclassifiable, this artist is best known for his hand-shaped furniture, but he also used butterfly, clock, and other whimsical motifs for chair backs.

able interiors were outfitted with sleek steel-and-glass furniture by Bauhaus-influenced designers and modulated with luxury fabrics and polished finishes. In America, the most up-to-the-minute new suburban homes were furnished with designs by Charles and Ray Eames, George Nelson, and others in the country's first generation of native-born Modernists, many of whom had taken new materials and production processes developed for the military and applied them to the manufacture of domestic goods. As the new designs were copied or modified for a wider market, they helped to spread the gospel of a new style. Modernism for the masses was pioneered by Habitat in London (the 1964 predecessor of Conran's) and IKEA (the Swedish company founded in 1958) but was not widely available for a broader market until the latter part of the century.

Of all the new modern designs, the easiest to win public acceptance were accessible furnishings by Danish designers and their contemporaries in the other Nordic nations. Scandinavian Modern furniture was made of natural-finished wood in sculptural forms, and arranged in rooms warmed with natural colors and touch-friendly textiles. Consumers seeking a liv-

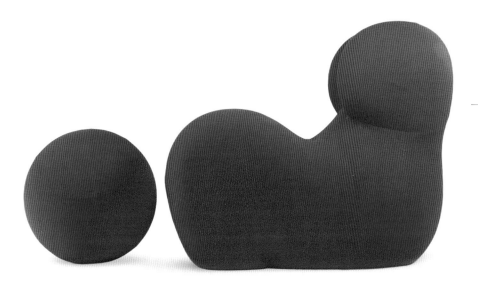

UP5 Chair and UP6 Ottoman
Gaetano Pesce (Italy)
1969
Stretch fabric, polyurethane foam, rubber

Seating designs that make the most of the flexibility of polyurethane foam. Shipped in a flat box, they expand to full size when unpacked. Included in Italy: The New Domestic Landscape exhibition and many museum collections.

able way to be modern embraced Scandinavian design and its creators—from Alvar Aalto to Hans Wegner, Finn Juhl, and their cabinetmaker-craftsmen colleagues in the 1950s and '60s—although its relatively conservative looks doomed it to a short reign as fashion forward. It was soon upstaged by attention-getting new pieces from Italy. Nurtured by Gio Ponti and the trend-setting *Domus* magazine, Joe Colombo, Mario Bellini, Achille Castiglioni, Gaetano Pesce, and their countrymen produced colorful, idiosyncratic designs for furniture and lighting that brought a fresh sense of fun to furnishings. In its lighthearted approach, Italian design challenged the seriousness and sameness of more conventional Modernism, foreshadowing its fall from favor. Although designers like Isamu Noguchi, Arne Jacobsen, Olivier Mourgue, and Vladimir Kagan designed furniture with curvilinear forms, and interior

Chaise Lounge, Charles and Ray Eames
(United States)
1968
Electrostatically coated aluminum,
foam, leather

With the familiar chaise silhouette, but an ultra-slim 18 inches wide, this was designed at the request of the Eameses' friend, film director Billy Wilder, who wanted a compact place for quick naps between takes. The husband-and-wife Eameses, who met at Cranbrook Academy of Art, are the most prominent American designers of the mid twentieth century.

designers tempered Modernism's sharp edges with historicist touches that made it more user-friendly, the cutting edge of Modernism was blunted by tedious and emotionless replications. Critics rebuked the style for its connotations of coldness, and a change in nomenclature from "Modern" to "Contemporary" failed to disguise the failings of formulaic architecture and impersonal interiors. The search would soon be on for an alternative.

Coconut Chair, George Nelson
& Associates (United States)
1955
Enameled metal, chrome-plated steel,
upholstery

A signature seating piece designed
when Nelson was director of design
for Herman Miller.

Ox Chair, Hans Wegner (Denmark)
1960
Molded polyurethane foam, leather,
matte chromed steel

Named for the animal its headrest
silhouette suggests, a recently revived
classic by one of the leading names in
Scandinavian furniture design.

Golliwog Planter, Erwine and
Estelle Laverne
(United States)
1961
Hand-painted aluminum,
wood, iron

One of a series of accessories—
these for lawn and patio—
reflecting the less-serious
approach to decorating in the
decade of pop and op art.

Karuselli Chair, Yrjö Kukkapuro (Finland)
1964
Fiberglass, leather, foam, chrome-plated steel

The fiberglass shell, supposedly inspired by the
shape of the designer's own body in a snowbank,
forms a cocoon enclosing the occupant. A trademark design by this Scandinavian master, it has
been in production for almost half a century.

Cone Chair, Verner Panton (Denmark)
1958
Chrome-plated steel, upholstery

The bold form and use of metal were,
at the time, radical departures from more
conservative Scandinavian styles.

Lamino Lounge Chair, Yngve Eckström
(Sweden)
1965
Birch plywood, upholstery

A classic midcentury design from Sweden,
during a time when most attention was given
to Danish furniture. It is still being made.

Safari Sofa, Archizoom Associati
(Italy)
1967
Lacquered fiberglass, upholstery

One of the most familiar designs by the
avant-garde Florence group (1966–74)
that, along with Superstudio(1966–78),
challenged the design establishment in
the attention-getting Superarchittetura
exhibitions (1966–67) of radical architecture. An empty room by Archizoom
was included in the Italy: The New
Domestic Landscape exhibition.

Dining Table, Warren Platner
(United States)
1966
Glass, enameled steel rods

From a collection including chairs,
tables, and ottomans, architect Platner
gives a light look to steel, shaping slim
rods into curved pedestals. A chair
from the collection was included in the
Design Since 1945 exhibition and its
accompanying publication.

HISTORICAL CONTEXT, 1970–2000

Orthodox Modernism, though only successful with the general public when applied in moderation, held its ground through much of the 1970s. Emerging from the aftermath of the Vietnam War, that decade was one of recovery and renewal in most of the Western world, and particularly in America. Despite the disruptions of Vietnam, the rebellion in Northern Ireland, the scandal of Watergate, and the problems of inflation and unemployment brought about by postwar recession, there was much to be optimistic about. Positive signs included the founding of Greenpeace, the first Earth Day, and the passing of the Equal Rights Amendment, the Endangered Species Act, and the Nuclear Proliferation Pact—all indicators of a growing concern for human rights and the welfare of the environment. The invention of the microprocessor and the introduction of home computers were the first steps in the technological changes that would revolutionize the design field and virtually erase national differences in design. In sharp contrast, an increasingly depersonalized society would stimulate the search for individuality, fostering entrepreneurship and the burgeoning craft movement. Fashion and pop culture fueled the freewheeling expressionism of psychedelic art, Andy Warhol's Factory, disco and Studio 54, ethnic dress and micro-to-maxi skirts. With the same sense of lightening, modern architecture and interiors showed signs of divergence from their usual iterations.

All fashions are doomed to fade, however, and the Modern movement was losing momentum. The 1980s proclaimed the demise, at least in its orthodox form, of an aesthetic that had reigned unchallenged for two decades. Despite its many critics, the high-profile Postmodern movement that followed helped propel design into a newsworthy subject of popular discourse. On other fronts, the decade was a contentious time

Louis 20 Side Chair, Philippe Starck (France)
1991
Polypropylene, aluminum
Made in limited quantities, this silhouette suggests the witty irreverence of Starck's furniture designs, all of which bear provocative names . . . this one suggesting the merger of classic French style with twentieth-century technology.

of radical styles and life-changing products: mass-market consumer electronics beginning in 1978 with the ubiquitous Sony Walkman, followed by MTV and GPS, Nintendo, Post-Its, digital cameras, and Apple's Macintosh. In a global context, the 1980s saw the fall of the Berlin Wall and the coining of the term "cyberspace." America continued its exploration of space, while back on the ground, free-spending yuppies spurred a vogue for designer labels that turned wearing apparel—and, later, household goods—into status symbols. Across the Atlantic, Beatlemania was succeeded by London's Youthquake, an atmosphere that encouraged the activities of avant-garde

young British designers who produced furniture that was topical, witty, and trendsetting. On a more serious side, the AIDS virus was discovered, cigarettes were proved hazardous to health, and Prozac was introduced to relieve the stresses of everyday life. Back in America, the decade ended with a recession that tempered its glittery excesses and slowed the pace of creative innovation.

As Postmodernism waned, design began to move along a less radical path. In the 1990s, a reevaluation of the century brought a wave of nostalgia and revivals of styles from decades

Coffee Table, Philip and Kelvin LaVerne (United States)
1965
Onyx, terrazzo, patinated bronze over pewter

The bronze top sits on a faceted base of solid pewter, the metals painstakingly aged and oxidized for several weeks by immersion in treated sand. The top is etched with images inspired by classical Asian artworks. Pieces by these father-and-son artisans were unique or in very limited production.

598 Lounge Chair and Ottoman
Pierre Paulin (France)
ca. 1970
Stretched fabric , enameled tubular steel

The so-called Groovy chair and other Paulin designs beginning with his 1966 Ribbon chair, replaced conventional upholstery with stretchy fabric over a flexible, tubular-steel frame—an innovation in seating construction. Paulin and Olivier Mourgue were France's most important contributors to avant-garde midcentury design.

past. Ready-to-wear also looked back, and vintage clothing began to rival marquee-name fashions, in a shift from trendiness to individual style. The universe was expanding with the launch of the Hubble Space Telescope, the International Space Station, and the discovery of a planet outside our solar system. It was also contracting, as borders between countries eroded with more international travel, the dissolution of the Soviet Union, and the signing of the European Treaty. Netscape and the World Wide Web enabled instant communication over vast distances; email became an addiction; and Google offered an unlimited source of information for anyone with a computer.

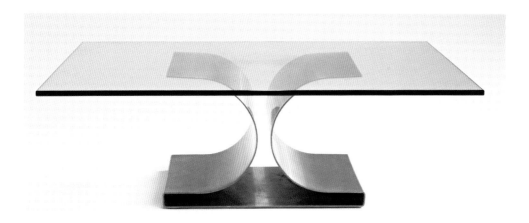

CAD and cybernetics were bringing a sea change to design, and the science of ergonomics, applied to commercial interiors and furniture, became an important consideration for a public increasingly concerned with health and fitness. Sharing the spotlight were esoteric influences like feng shui and holistic design—Zen principles applied to interiors. Japanese fashion innovators such as Rei Kawakubo and Issey Miyake found that a coterie of consumers were adventurous enough to wear iconoclastic design, and other new styles drew inspiration from exotic lands as well as traditional Western sources.

X-Base Coffee Table, Michel Boyer
(France)
1968
Stainless steel, glass
Like Maria Pergay, Boyer was one of the early designers, many in France, to explore the use of stainless steel in furniture.

This openness to diversity reflected the multiculturalism of modern society, which had engendered a desire for self-expression. It was becoming apparent that design was one way to achieve it.

Design was also expanding its mission to take on a sense of responsibility to society and the world: Victor Papanek's 1972 book *Design for the Real World: Human Ecology and Social Change* suggested that design could help contribute to a better life and could deal with social needs. The 1990 Americans with Disabilities Act prescribed standards of accessibility

for buildings and interiors. And the stringent Clean Air Act of 1993 was a precursor to the sustainability movement that would rewrite the ground rules in all areas of design. To an increasingly overburdened society, Minimalism's penchant for deaccession rather than acquisition seemed appropriate—though heightened public interest in design meant that there was room for more than one player in the style-setting game. On the eve of the millennium, the design climate was increasingly permissive, and Modernism's identity was continually challenged—and increasingly vague.

Ring Chair, Maria Pergay (France)
1970
Polished stainless steel

Probably the most famous of Pergay's designs, in a form that contradicts the rigidity of steel with a ribbon-like, flexible form. Asked to develop new applications by a producer of stainless steel, a material then used only in industry, Pergay devised her own tools to transform it into elegant, sculptural furniture, made individually in small editions.

Bilobato Coffee Table
Angelo Mangiarotti (Italy)
1971
Marble

WHAT'S IN A NAME?
THE SEVERAL
CONTRADICTIONS
OF MODERNISM

Within a period of several decades, Modernism moved from a clearly defined aesthetic to one almost impossible to pin down. Traditionally, styles were identified by characteristic silhouettes, specific materials, fabrication techniques, and ornamental motifs. The same was true, for the most part, for premodern movements such as Arts & Crafts and Art Nouveau, Vienna Secessionism and Glasgow Style. But from its full flowering at the Bauhaus and subsequent manifestations in many countries, Modernism unshackled itself from history, eschewing inspiration from the past. This effort to free design from formulas, however, proved as restrictive as the traditions it rejected. Applied with single-minded precision, it stifled ingenuity and produced look-alike buildings, cookie-cutter furniture, and boring interiors. Sharply criticized and ultimately rejected, Modernism was replaced by several postmodern movements (including the one bearing that name). Architects and designers cast their nets wide in search of a new direction. They sought to recapture individuality while meeting the challenges of advancing technology and changing social needs. To do this, they took a variety of approaches, along disparate paths, with remarkably different results—and with unequal degrees of success.

The resulting interiors and furnishings were on the one hand spare and architectural, or on the other purely decorative. Despite this apparent disjunction, the aims of designers in the postmodern era remained consistent with the original Bauhaus tenets—designing for the machine, using modern materials, and placing function before form—but with some important qualifications. Their embrace of industrialization,

Navy Chair, United States Navy
1944
Aluminum

Workaday seating designed for use on naval vessels became a Modernist basic recently transposed into a sustainable twenty-first-century design in a fabrication using discarded soda bottles.

with its benefits of mass production and affordable objects, was tempered with a respect for craft and the handmade; their exploration of man-made materials was partnered with a new search for environmentally sensitive ones; they considered functionalism desirable but not always more important than visual statements; and, with continued ambivalence about the presence of ornament, they often amended its exclusion to

allow decoration for its own sake. Nevertheless, an underlying agreement of objectives gave coherence and consistency to the designs of this era—even the most decorative of them can justifiably be labeled Modern.

There were two factors that confused the issue. Throughout the history of design—from the ancient world to medieval times, from the Renaissance to eighteenth-century France and England—styles had been set by autocratic rulers, heads of churches, or the nobility. In the nineteenth century, reformers and intellectuals assumed that role, reevaluating design stan-

Scimitar Lounge Chair
Preben Fabricius and Jørgen Kastholm
(Denmark)
1962
Stainless steel, leather

Perhaps ahead of its time, this chair broke with the familiar Scandinavian Modern aesthetic of sculptural forms in natural wood. Unlike most of their countrymen at the time, Fabricius & Kastholm conceived spare, minimalist furniture that was more closely related to the functionalist approach of Bauhaus designers.

DF-2000 Cabinet, Raymond Loewy
(United States)
1960
Plastic, laminate, enameled aluminum

One of the pioneers of the new field of industrial design in the 1930s, Loewy was attempting here to add style to production furniture made of low-cost modern materials.

dards and initiating revivals of historic styles. In the twentieth century, however, an increasingly democratic culture—socially, if not politically—moved design leadership to a still broader field, played on by tastemakers from several directions. At one side of the spectrum, architects and designers, artists, writers, and critics, and on the other side, celebrities and fashion leaders, dictated to a public eager to follow the latest fashions. Every individual was free to pursue a path defined by instinct, self-expression, or personal taste. The result, in the closing decades, was rampant eclecticism and the confusion of defining design labels.

Another change was potentially even more disruptive. Contemporary interiors were no longer derived from, or even necessarily related to, architecture. From the first flowering of the practice in the Renaissance, architects had not only designed buildings but almost always determined the interiors and furnishings within them as well. This changed, particularly in America, as interior design developed into a professional practice of specialists responsible only for the areas inside a building, and modern architecture introduced a "blank slate" of adaptable, flat-walled spaces mandating no specific deco-

Jumbo Coffee Table, Gae Aulenti
(Italy)
1964
Marble

A classic from midcentury Italy by Aulenti, an architect and one of the Italian innovators featured in Italy: The New Domestic Landscape. She was the art director of the influential magazine *Casabella* from the mid-1950s to the mid-1960s and in 1986 was named a Chevalier of the Légion d'honneur for her design of the Musée d'Orsay interiors in Paris.

Floor Lamp, Philip Johnson
and Richard Kelly (United States)
1968
Enameled bronze, enameled aluminum

rative style. Unrestricted by architectural surrounds, modern interiors could be entirely individualistic. A cohort of practitioners arose to execute them: architects and interior designers, supplemented by furniture and accessory designers, color and lighting consultants, art advisors, and other experts who

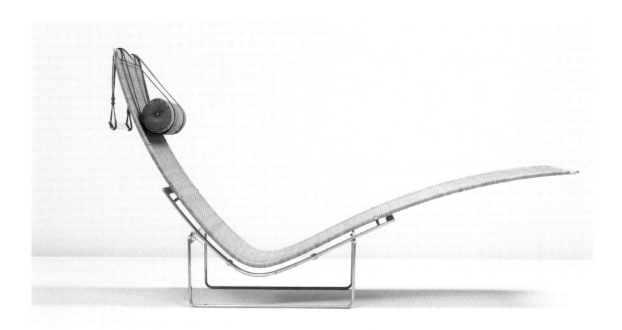

together determined the design of interior space. These specialists traveled on parallel but not necessarily congruent paths—occasionally colliding, with sometimes unfortunate results.

This many-cooks-at-the-broth situation further complicated the definition of modern styles in the last decades of the twentieth century. Despite the presence of several clear and sometimes-overlapping directions, no single aesthetic was universally adopted. Much of the ambivalence can be seen as a response to, or a rebellion against, the midcentury definition of Modernism.

Chaise, Poul Kjærholm (Denmark)
1965
Stainless steel, wicker, leather
Inspired by the classic Rococo chaise form, this has a similar curving silhouette but entirely independent elements: the body and base are held together only by gravity and friction.

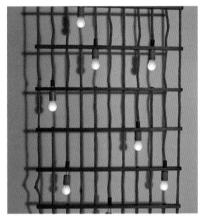

Dome 2 Chair, Asko Lax (Finland)
1999
Molded plywood, matte or
chrome-plated steel

Rope Lamp, Temde (Germany)
ca. 1970s
Walnut, rope, ceramic

Cocktail Table, Paul Evans
(United States)
1973
Sculpted and painted steel, plate glass

Evans's variations on metal furniture

included custom pieces with textured and
sculpted surfaces and applications of tone-
on-tone color.

Golgotha Chair, Gaetano Pesce (Italy)
1972
Fiberglass with Dacron fiberfill,
polyester resin

Treating design as a kind of performance,
this was the first chair made in the "diversi-
fied series" technique, using flexible molds
that could be manipulated in production,
with the emerging object then stiffened
with resin. The fabricator becomes part

of the design process, and each piece
is unique, contraverting the concept of
standardized production. Pesce's work
often introduces random elements, making
the final product somewhat unpredictable,
even to its creator.

X-Leg Table, John Dickinson
(United States)
1980
Painted plaster

An anthropomorphic work by a designer
known for his idiosyncratic pieces that
emulate natural forms.

The end of the century was unlike any period in history, prefiguring the quixotic nature of current design, which has several aspects and a handful of labels and has become a heterogeneous category incorporating art, craft, and sculpture. At this writing, there have never been so many variants of Modernism in architecture, interiors, and especially objects. Much of what we find acceptable today would have been scoffed at, cast aside, or given another label a quarter-century or even just a decade past. With these radical changes in design, the very definition of Modernism has been challenged to take on new and broader meaning.

Oh! Chair, Karim Rashid
(United States, b. Egypt)
1999
Polypropylene, steel, nylon

The curves and cutouts of this mass-produced chair reflect the fondness for organic forms often seen in the work of a designer who made the Garbo waste-basket into a fashion statement. Winner of an IDEA silver award and shown in many museum collections, Rashid is one of the most prolific designers of his generation, with more than three thousand products to his credit, including interiors, lighting, and packaging designs.

Tube Chair, Joe Colombo (Italy)
1969
Arcipiuma plastic with coated foam upholstery, steel, and rubber clips

One of the innovative designs shown in exhibitions Italy: The New Domestic Landscape and Design Since 1945 and in the collection of the Metropolitan Museum of Art, the Museum of Modern Art, and many others. The tubular sections can be rearranged for varying seating positions or nested into one unit for shipping.

THE HERITAGE
OF NATIONALISM

Every era in history is defined by what is new, but every country must come to terms with, and accommodate, its own past. In the course of the twentieth century, an increasingly global

culture and a revolution in communications gradually erased the barriers between nations, eliminating many of the differentiations between styles. Even more than the other arts, architecture and design have reflected folk tradition and expressed national identity. Although these traditions are no longer as prevalent, traces still remain—sometimes in architectural or furniture forms, sometimes in ornamental motifs, and almost invariably in the decoration of interiors.

Born in Germany, the Bauhaus was perhaps the most influential leveler of design, and its then-radical innovations continue to influence the way Modernism is viewed today.

Leonardo Sofa, Francesco Audrito and Athena Sampaniotou (Italy)
1969
Rubber-coated polyurethane

Silla Mariposa Chair
Pedro Friedeberg (Mexico, b. Italy)
1965
Carved, lacquered, and gilded Mexican mahogany

Friedeberg's witty and instantly recognizable designs are fantasy forms—and altogether impossible to designate as belonging to any style.

Though criticized as too doctrinaire in its precepts, it provided a universal and democratic foundation for a new direction in Modernism. Declaring the decorative arts and crafts equal to the fine arts, and embracing industrialization, it set the stage for the defining image of twentieth-century architecture: the International Style. In contrast to this functionalist ethic, the French tradition was one of elitist design and luxury handcraft. Art Deco, an attempt to translate these principles to a modern vocabulary, was superseded by the machine-age aesthetic, but its ideals have been resurrected in today's one-off and limited-edition furniture.

Malitte, Roberto Sebastian Matta (Chile)
1966
Wool fabric over polyurethane foam

Featured in the exhibitions Italy: The New Domestic Landscape, Design Since 1945, and Design 1935-1965: environment plays with a new material—polyfoam—with a puzzle-like assemblage of three chairs, a bench, and a cube combined into a square, and arrangeable in different configurations. It was originally commissioned by the furniture manufacturer Dino Gavina.

The middle decades of the twentieth century brought the last, and probably the most influential, expressions of national style. Scandinavian designers pioneered a populist approach to modernity, commingling craft traditions and natural materials with machine production in furniture that was easy to look at, pleasant to touch, and comfortable to use. Proselytizing the importance of good design for everyone, Scandinavian design appealed to a broad audience and encouraged higher standards in design, even for quotidian objects.

The first generation of American-born designers—excepting Frank Lloyd Wright, who was always ahead of his time—came to prominence at midcentury, most of them trained

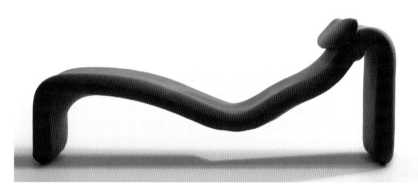

by European expatriates. Adopting defense-industry materials and new technology, they put war-production capabilities to peacetime applications in mass-produced furnishings.

Responding to a less-fortunate postwar situation, Italian designers dealt with decimated factories and raw materials shortages. They made the most out of very little, with risk-taking, unconventional objects in provocative shapes, bright colors, and unglamorous materials, energizing the market and introducing the idea that furniture and lighting could be fun.

And in Japan, the centuries-old heritage of refined minimalism was filtered through the lens of Modernism in East-

Djinn Chaise, Olivier Mourgue
(France)
1965
Upholstery, chrome-plated steel
The most celebrated design by a master of organic form and technically innovative seating concepts.

Floor Lamp, Isamu Noguchi
(United States)
ca. 1975
Enameled steel, paper
One of a series of Shoji-paper lighting designs called Akari, after a Japanese word designating light and brightness. Made in many shapes and sizes, they are often referred to as light sculptures. Noguchi, a Japanese-American artist and designer best known for his sculptures and public works of landscape architecture, also designed several celebrated pieces of furniture.

meets-West translations of the aesthetic. These and other elements retained from the diverse histories of a multicultural society continue to inform today's varied and vital forms of modern design, but they are increasingly difficult to isolate.

With the evaporation of national borders, the characteristics that once distinguished the design of one country from that of another have dissipated; not all objects with whimsical forms and lively colors come from Italy, not all those of natural materials and warm woods are Scandinavian, not all that merge functionality and mass-market production originate in America. The result was, and continues to be, a degree of

homogeneity in modern global style. At the same time, cross-cultural communication has encouraged creativity across borders; innovative ideas, once limited to a few design centers, now emanate from almost every corner of the world.

Mischievous Chair and Ottoman
Sergio Rodrigues (Brazil)
1963
Leather, rosewood

Transposing a classic Colonial form in local wood and leather this designer's furniture helped create a distinctive identity for Brazilian modern design. He collaborated frequently with architect Oscar Niemeyer.

Lumikiik Self-Balancing Table Lamp
François Dallegret (France)
1970
Aluminum, opaque Perspex

This toy-like form was a limited edition of three, plus two artists' proofs.

Orgone Chaise, Marc Newson
(Australia)
2000
Lacquered fiberglass

Newson continues to work with the
biomorphic forms that have inspired
him since the 1980s, now with
advanced materials and space-age
technology. He has used these recently
to design transportation vehicles:
surfboard, boat, space plane. The
designer has made the same silhouette
in polished aluminum, felt, wicker,
and wetsuit fabric.

Gherpe Table Lamp, Superstudio
(Italy)
1967
Plastic, aluminum

More decorative than functional, this
lamp flouts conventional form with
curves of colorful plastic. Superstudio (1966–78) was one of the radical
Florence-based groups of young
designers whose pop-influenced
Anti-Design work prefigured that
of Memphis.

MOVEMENTS AFTER MODERNISM

As the Modern movement floundered, it elicited comparisons to its most maligned predecessors: in 1970 historian Mark Girouard declared it to be "as doctrinaire and intolerant in its day as the Gothic Revival." Once hailed for its individuality, orthodox Modernism produced a monotonous succession of

copycat International Style structures that turned functional form into formula. The curtain-walled, glass-box architecture that punctuated city skylines and proliferated across suburban landscapes had become as predictable as the period styles it had cast aside. Equally predictable were its sparely furnished, neutral-schemed interiors with their rubber-stamp arrangements of virtually identical furniture. Modernism's fresh new face proved to be a shallow facade: applied according to the rule, it was sterile, meaningless, and even worse, dull. Looser interpretations failed to mitigate the backlash against an aesthetic that was perceived as lacking context or connection to its users.

Arco Floor Lamp, Achille & Pier Giacomo Castiglioni (Italy)
1962
Carrara marble, chrome-plated steel, aluminum
Classic marble paired with contemporary steel and aluminum, the extended arc suspends the lighting source over a surface several feet from the base. An icon of Italian Modernism, shown in the landmark exhibitions Italy: The New Domestic Landscape, Design Since 1945, and Design 1935–1965:

What Modern Was, and a fixture (often accompanying Barcelona chair-and-table ensembles) in countless International Style interiors. The Castiglioni brothers designed many of the most celebrated Italian lighting designs as well as furniture and accessories.

Ateljee, Yrjö Kukkapuro (Finland)
1964
Steel tubing, birch or black-stained plywood, detachable upholstery and cushions

The canon of Modernism had actually raised doubts as early as the 1960s, and alternative directions emerged in the decade that followed. The humanism of Scandinavian design was one influence, but the most dramatic was the explosion of originality when Italian design took center stage, and Milan became the nucleus of the design world. The Museum of Mod-

ern Art's landmark 1972 exhibition *Italy: The New Domestic Landscape* highlighted the forward-thinking ideas of its imaginative designers and permissive producers. Their attention-getting furniture and lighting intrigued the public and challenged conventional practitioners, opening the doors to others seeking a way to make design relevant.

The obvious solution to some was a healthy infusion of the past. Classical references in many and varied forms proliferated in Postmodernism, a style defined by contextualism, historicism, and ornamentation. Robert Venturi, in his books *Complexity and Contradiction in Architecture* (1966) and

Boalum Lamp, Livio Castiglioni and Gianfranco Frattini (Italy)
1969
Translucent reinforced plastic tubing, metal rings, thermoplastic ends, incandescent bulbs

The user determines the form of this pop-influenced lighting unit, which can be used on floor, wall, or table, and can be assembled into units up to 8 feet long. Shown in the exhibition *Italy: The New Domestic Landscape,* it has become a classic example of ingenuity in lighting design.

Balans, Peter Opsvik (Norway)
1979
Fabric, foam, steel

One of many variations of a "kneeling chair," a seating concept designed to promote optimum spinal alignment, with thighs at an angle and shins helping to support body weight. Opsvik is equally famous for his adjustable "Tripp Trapp" child's seat.

Learning from Las Vegas (1972), was the standard-bearer for the new vision, which produced buildings that reveled in the familiarity of traditional forms and paid homage to the ancient world and the eighteenth century. Seeking to return architecture to its role as a means of communication, Postmodernism applied classical motifs and bold colors in witty, spontaneous effects that relieved the monotony of Modern buildings. Provocative and often charming in architecture, Postmodernism translated awkwardly into furniture and often approached the bizarre when applied to interior design. It was therefore short-lived, but it was an important landmark in design history,

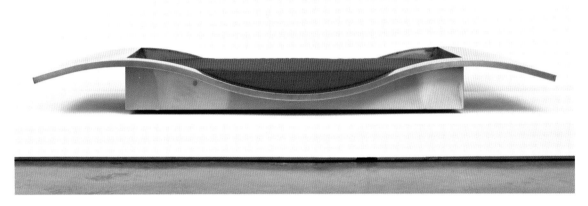

shining a spotlight on the failings of the style against which it rebelled.

Another movement, Deconstructivism, seized on the symmetry of International Style architecture as its most egregious error, replacing it with exploded structures of aggressively asymmetrical form and staccato linear shapes—no two precisely alike. It was architecture in pursuit of anarchy, more extreme in execution than was conceived in James Wines's *De-Architecture* (1987). Frank Gehry, Rem Koolhaas, Daniel Libeskind, and Zaha Hadid were among its early practitioners. In this radical style, interior walls might angle, ceilings slope,

Flying Carpet Daybed, Maria Pergay (France)
1968
Uginox stainless steel, fabric

Stainless steel, treated like a textile, is shaped into sensual form by a designer who began her career making silver decorative accessories. Like all of her pieces, this early work was made individually and in small editions—generally no more than forty.

windows punctuate walls in varied shapes and no particular pattern. This disjuncture of volumes produced interiors that were always arresting, and usually intriguing, but sometimes suggested novelty for its own sake. In such surroundings, furnishings played a subsidiary role: architecture upstaged decoration. Instead of providing the frame for a *gesamtkunstwerk*—an interior as a total work of art—architecture became the art in its entirety. Spaces like this were often difficult to live in.

Minimalism, the most rigorous of the breakaway movements—pioneered by architect John Pawson—stripped archi-

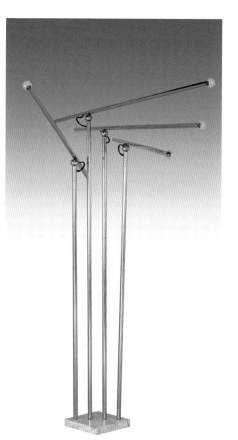

tecture and interiors down to their barest bones, eschewing distractions in spaces that were highly disciplined constructs of volume and form. Interiors were primarily black-and-white and sparingly furnished, with rigorously edited arrangements of rectilinear furniture, few accessories, and absolutely no pattern. The look was not merely pared down but almost naked.

Related to Minimalism and leading into it, another reaction against formulaic Modernism took the movement's reverence for technology literally, evoking a factory aesthetic in interiors furnished with industrial, medical, and commercial equipment. It adopted the label of High-Tech, after a 1978

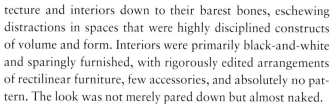

Mies Lounge Chair and Ottoman
Archizoom Associati (Italy)
1969
Chrome-plated steel, rubber, pony skin, electrical components (for the ottoman)

A cheeky commentary on functionalism with rubber-sling seat and illuminated footrest.

Floor Lamp with Four Rotating Arms, Gino Sarfatti (Italy)
c. 1960
Tubular steel, marble base

Table Lamp on Wheels
Martine Bedin (Italy)
1981
Enameled metal

Postmodernism in an accent piece
from the Memphis collaborative.

Desk, Arthur Espenet Carpenter
(United States)
1968
American black walnut with cherry
drawers

Self-taught Carpenter (known profes-
sionally as Espenet) was one of the
second generation of American studio
craftsmen. His skillfully executed pieces
helped to elevate the status of handcraft
to that of an art. He was featured in the
1972 Woodenworks exhibition at the
Renwick Gallery and many exhibitions
thereafter.

Plia Chair, Giancarlo Piretti (Italy)
1969
Chrome-plated steel, aluminum, Lucite

The first folding chair made in plastic
and one of the most successful of all
Italian midcentury designs, it has sold
millions since its introduction more
than four decades ago. In addition
to being comfortable and eminently
functional, its award-winning good
looks have placed it in major museum
collections, including the Museum of
Modern Art.

book of the same name, and flourished as the accepted style of furnishing for lofts and loft-emulating interiors. High Tech was most avant-garde in its architectural applications—such as the skeletal exterior of Rogers and Foster's Centre Pompidou (1987), which has been called both High-Tech and Postmodern. In the same period, California architects such as Eric Owen Moss and Thomas Mayne created aberrant structures that defied definition by these, or any specific, labels.

The polar opposite of such radical directions, but equally strong in its rebellion against conventional Modernism, was

the Studio Craft movement, which was born in the 1960s and flourished in the ensuing decades. It arose in opposition to the proliferation of machine-made objects, not disparaging their quality (as had the Arts & Crafts movement) but challenging their lack of individuality. Handcrafted furniture by Wharton Esherick, George Nakashima, Sam Maloof, Wendell Castle, and others offered sophisticated alternatives to machine-made goods, prefiguring the redefinition of one-off pieces as a crossover category of design/art.

Along with the rebellious, but still modern, movements, the late twentieth century saw the return of styles that were

FK 87 Grasshopper Lounge Chair
Preben Fabricius and Jørgen Kastholm (Denmark)
1968
Matte chrome-plated steel, canvas, leather

Sedia 1, Enzo Mari (Italy)
1974
Unfinished pine
Sophisticated do-it-yourself design: delivered as precut boards, with nails and instructions that allow the consumer to build the chair using only a hammer.

literally historicist. A revival of Arts & Crafts was generated by museum exhibitions, bracketed by the influential Arts & Crafts Movement in America, 1876–1916 at Princeton Uni-

versity in 1972 and the Museum of Fine Arts Boston's 1987 exhibition Art That Is Life: The Arts & Crafts Movement in America, 1875–1920. At the other extreme was a revival of Art Deco, a style that came to public attention after a 1971 exhibition of the same name at the Minneapolis Institute of Arts. (The term had been coined by Bevis Hillier in his 1968 book *Art Deco of the 20s and 30s*, after the 1925 Paris Exposition des Arts Décoratifs et Industriels Modernes.) The return of this elitist style and its labor-intensive objects inspired interiors that incorporated iconic 1920s French furniture into otherwise modern surroundings, catapulting the

Music Stand, Sam Maloof
(United States)
1970
Carved walnut

A trademark design by a first-generation, self-taught studio craftsman whose work was featured at the 1962 Seattle World's Fair and has been seen in museum exhibitions as well.

Rocking Chair, Arthur Espenet Carpenter (United States)
1970
Laminated and carved walnut, upholstery

Several of the early studio craftsmen made rockers—perhaps reflecting the movement's nostalgia and the rejection of machine-made, mass-produced forms. A unique piece, this is one of Carpenter's most original, and most distinctive, works.

most masterful pieces to the status of six-figure, collectible treasures. Looking further back, the Museum of Modern Art mounted Vienna 1900: Art, Architecture and Design in 1986, spurring the rediscovery of the graphic modernism of the Wiener Werkstatte era. Objects from these early modern periods, despite their contrasting aesthetics, were compatible with Modernist furniture and could be introduced to soften the severity of industrial-age interiors.

The appeal of handwork notwithstanding, technology remained a dominant element in design. The opening of the exhibition The Machine Age in America, 1918–1941 at the

Brooklyn Museum in 1986 encouraged the fascination with industrial design and the machine aesthetic that had been reflected in High Tech and its quirky but individualistic interiors.

Beginning in the 1960s and increasingly in the following decades, the relatively new science of ergonomics directed designers to consider comfort and musculoskeletal requirements. This sometimes led to technical and medical issues overtaking a concern for visual appeal in the creation of new furniture (beginning with executive office chairs and task seating). As the science evolved, ergonomics entered the home

Modular Seating, Ueli Berger, Eleanora Peduzzi-Riva, and Heinze Ulrich (Switzerland)
1970
Leather, reinforced molded foam, wood, zippers

One of the most original ideas to emerge from postwar Italy was the endlessly expandable modular sofa. This is among the most familiar examples of the genre. A similar design by Cini Boeri was shown in the exhibition Italy: The New Domestic Landscape.

and has evolved into what is now called universal design—a movement based less on aesthetics than on social welfare and human needs.

Less revolutionary but steadily gaining ground, the development of multipurpose designs in furniture was important to the growing numbers of apartment-dwelling consumers and those faced with smaller living spaces in the postindustrial society. The same considerations propelled the growth of what was first called "knock-down" and later (more appealingly) "ready-to-assemble" furniture, which was made internationally acceptable by the pioneering Swedish-based retailer IKEA.

The most notable revival in the wave of end-of-century nostalgia was a relatively recent one: midcentury design. Three decades after its first appearance, it returned, encouraged by the imprimatur of major museum exhibitions: Design Since 1945 at the Philadelphia Museum of Art in 1983, and Design 1935–1965: What Modern Was at Montreal's Musée des Arts Decoratifs in 1991. And in 1987 the Metropolitan Museum of Art, inaugurating its Lila Acheson Wallace Wing, included a permanent gallery for modern design. Followed by an important publication—*Modern Design in the Metropolitan Museum of Art, 1890–1990* by the curator R. Craig Miller—

Campus Chair, Johannes Foersom and Peter Hiort-Lorenzen (Denmark)
1992
Polished or powder-coated chrome, wood veneer, laminate or upholstered seat and back

PK 54 Round Dining Table
Poul Kjærholm (Denmark)
1972
Porsgrunn marble, chrome-plated steel frame, maple

An elegant solution to the expandable table, with six arc-shaped leaves that attach to its perimeter, forming a decorative border. When not in use, the leaves sit in their own storage stand.

it was an influential acknowledgment that the many faces of Modernism, despite its defects and its convoluted history, had become part of the design vernacular.

The final decade of the century saw relatively little change in the direction of design, without any new movements or even dominating trends. It was more a time of absorbing the development of the preceding years than one of breaking new ground. As the millennium approached, the newly inclusive attitude enabled myriad style options as well as reinterpretations of the recent past. Preservationists and revivalists shared the design stage with aficionados of the avant-garde, delighting fashion followers and confounding trend forecasters and critics. Some of the most innovative architectural environments of these years incorporated furnishings that, though some half-century old, still look indisputably current. In an unfortunate corollary, these iconic objects have inspired any number of designs that pay them homage but most of which fall far short of the finesse of the originals.

On the other hand, many recent interiors—indeed, many of the past half-century—have continued to reprise classical and eighteenth-century design, eschewing the understatement and the perceived severity of Modernism. Notwithstanding their choice of period furnishings, the designers of these spaces broke with tradition in their use of unconventional palettes, unpredictable pattern mixes, and idiosyncratic choices of ornament and accessories; historical accuracy was secondary to visual effect. The best of such interiors were soigné and sophisticated; the worst inclined toward ostentation, but they too have a place—though a corollary one—in the narrative of Modernism. And despite its much-heralded demise, the International Style (and its prime progenitor, Mies van der Rohe) continued to cast a compelling shadow on the landscape of design. This was acknowledged by the Museum of Modern Art and the Whitney Museum of American Art in a groundbreaking joint venture, Mies in Berlin (at MoMA) and Mies in America (at the Whitney) in 2001, recalling for the new century Modernism's great achievements in the last.

DESIGN AFTER MODERNISM

Universale Chairs, Joe Colombo (Italy)
1965
Coated ABS plastic
The first adult-size injection-molded chair made of ABS plastic, a new material at the time, reflecting the risk-taking attitude of designers and producers in postwar Italy.

Paramount Table Lamp, Gruppo UFO
(Italy)
1970
Glazed ceramic, nylon, chrome-plated metal

From a collection entitled bau. haus 1, probably a tongue-in-cheek homage to the far
more straitlaced Bauhaus.

Swivel Coffee Table with Five Bumps
Wendell Castle (United States)
1969
Gel-coated fiberglass

From a collection called the Molar Group,
an exploration in molded fiberglass by a
designer best known for his handcrafted
wood furniture.

S 70 Barstool, Börge Lindau and
Bo Lindekrantz (Sweden)
1968
Chrome-plated or powder-coated steel,
birch or upholstery

Pyramid, Shiro Kuramata (Japan)
1968
Transparent and black acrylic resin,
casters

A whimsical but functional storage unit,
with seventeen variably sized drawers,
prefigures the classical references in
Kuramata's later designs as a member
of the Memphis collaborative. Its sibling,
a rectilinear column, has drawers that
revolve around a center pole. Kuramata
designed several hundred restaurant and
bar interiors, but he is best known for his
unconventional furniture designs.

Magic Cube Table, Gabriella Crespi (Italy)
1970
Stainless steel

Working in many different materials, Crespi made elegant furniture and accessories of brass, wood, marble, and steel, often adorned with shells and jewels. Concerned with multifunctionality, she designed tables that changed height and pieces that opened for storage, patenting the mechanisms that, thanks to her architectural training, she devised.

Table, Willy Rizzo (Italy)
1970
Aluminum, lacquered wood

Tom-Vac Chair, Ron Arad
(United Kingdom, b. Israel)
1996
Dyed-through polypropylene, chrome-plated steel

One of Arad's relatively few designs for mass production. Light and stackable with a flexible corrugated seat. Seen in the exhibition European Design Since 1985: Shaping the New Century.

TOWARD THE
TWENTY-FIRST CENTURY:
TRANSFORMATION AND
REGENERATION

As "modern" was transposed from an adjective into a noun, Modern and Modernism came to define a specific style—a style of the moment. And as with all styles, its moment would inevitably pass. But in the early years of the new millennium, Modernism has been born anew. Transformed from its original incarnation, Modernism has embraced different and broader definitions, encompassing a panoply of comfortably coexisting interpretations. Style variations are multicultural and geographically limitless: in the digitally sophisticated global community, ideas are disseminated instantly from country to country—in design as in science, technology, and all the arts.

Planka, Börge Lindau and
Bo Lindecrantz (Sweden)
1985
Lacquered plywood, perforated sheet
metal or leather sling, chrome tubing,
upholstered foam

Something of a classic, this has been in production since it was first introduced. It adjusts to the user's height via a moving headrest.

Stuffed Seating, Jay Stanger
(United States)
1989
Colored leather and anodized
aluminum

Artwork that functions, by a designer whose use of lively colors and provocative silhouettes suggests an affinity with pop art and Postmodern design.

This explosion of creative output disdains limitation by labels; to paraphrase a familiar comment about art, it's design if you say it's design. Architecture is still being created by architects, but thanks to computer modeling, they are finding new ways of designing buildings: devising coiled, folded, and abstracted forms and executing them in both existing and newly discov-

ered materials, often using techniques borrowed from other industries.

In furniture design and fabrication, the changes are perhaps even more striking. The best of the newest modern design—and there is a considerable amount of it—can come from anywhere, be made with any available material or technique, and take almost any conceivable shape. Some of it may not even be recognizable as furniture. Where functionalism once propelled design, experimentation or emotion now often dominates: the idea behind a design is often as important as, and sometimes more important than, the design itself.

Bend Sofa, Patricia Urquiola (Spain)
2010
Wool fabric, flexible cold-shaped foam, tubular steel

Maralunga, Vico Magistretti (Italy)
1973
Steel, black plastic, polyurethane foam and polyester, fabric or leather

Perhaps the future will bring a new and more descriptive name for this heterogeneous era, but for the present it is best described as a transformation and regeneration of the Modernism that was.

There is today more forward-looking than retrograde design, and still more can be anticipated in the years to come, as next-generation computer capabilities, experiments with materials and technology, and advances in construction continue to transform the appearance and composition of buildings and furniture. The pace of change continues to accelerate at astonishing speed. Today's design studios are more like laboratories, and such arcane terms as motion-capture and rapid prototyping, electrolytic baths, and thermoplastics have become part of the design vocabulary. Some of the experimental works are more aberrant than unique, but along with those have come genuine accomplishments. Significantly, these explorations into new territory have also given rise to a new category, that of design/art, marking the erosion of the barriers that once separated the two. Furniture has become not only an expression of our culture—as it has always been—but also a new art form that can simultaneously please the eye, engage the intellect, and stimulate the emotions.

Designers are more inclined than ever before to break rules, push envelopes, and strike out in new directions. This is all to the good. Better still, issues of social responsibility are now accepted as integral to the designer's role, with the expectation that, beyond simply enhancing our surroundings, design can help improve the world for its inhabitants.

Where will the next direction-marker point? That is not yet clear, but the present mélange of styles and the democratic approach to design augur a revived, reenergized, enduring form of Modernism or, even more intriguing, something light-years beyond.

Klassenraumstuhl, Stefan Wewerka
(Germany)
1970
Lacquered wood
A tongue-in-cheek design that prefigures
the design/art objects of later decades.
Made in an edition of forty.

MIDCENTURY

The prototypical midcentury interior exemplified the ideal of "Good Design" as defined by standard-setters like the Museum of Modern Art. A neutral-tone background sets off clean-lined furniture, most of it designed by American-born Modernists. Among the classics here are a George Nelson sofa, Charles and Ray Eames chairs, a Mies van der Rohe daybed, and an Isamu Noguchi coffee table in the living area. In the dining area are Harry Bertoia Diamond chairs; and on the balcony level are an Eames lounge chair and storage units.

PRELUDE: REIGNING MODERNISM, 1950-1970

The golden years of Modernism in its purest form lasted a scant two decades, but the aesthetic it established would be modified, mutated, rejected, and finally transformed and resurrected within a period of a quarter-century. Beyond the costs in human life and physical destruction, the Second World War wreaked dramatic changes in the economic and social structures of the countries involved, directly or indirectly. Some of these changes altered the climate of design, encouraging the search for an appropriate new aesthetic.

Corona Chair, Poul Volther
(Denmark) 1961
Fabric or leather, polyurethane
foam, matte chromed steel

Rope Table, John Dickinson
(United States)
1970
Painted plaster

This San Francisco interior designer
made many variants of the theme
of faux–draped and tied occasional
tables and stools.

Bel Aire Chair, Peter Shire (United States)
1982
Fabric upholstery, foam, wood

Brilliant color and jaggedly abstract shapes in
the Postmodern mode, from a California-based
artist who worked with the Memphis group in
Milan. Shire's best known works are in ceramics—particularly the colorful, whimsical
teapots he has been making for almost four
decades—though he has made decorative
objects in metal and glass, as well as furniture
and public sculptures.

Chandelier, Stilnovo (Italy)
1960
Brass, enameled steel, glass

Lily Lounge Chair, Erwine and
Estelle Laverne (United States)
1967
Perspex, fabric-covered cushion

See-through plastic in shapely curvilinear
forms helped bring a workaday material
into high fashion. One of this series, the
Lily, was featured in Design Since 1945.
The Lavernes, husband and wife, became
celebrated for their transparent seating.

Good design began to filter down from the province of privilege to a more democratic entitlement for everyone who wanted it. The 1950s, a time of restoration and rebuilding, were also a time of economic recovery for the Allied nations, particularly the United States. The conservatism of the early postwar years shifted quickly into active, upbeat postwar building and economic prosperity, the race to conquer space, beatniks, the baby boom, and rock and roll—all contributing to an enthusiasm that fed creativity, encouraging the growing ranks of homegrown designers. The civil rights and women's liberation movements in the 1960s ushered in an atti-

tude of greater tolerance, and the appropriately democratic designs of what is now called "Midcentury Modernism"— simple furniture, affordable prices—were perfectly suited to the time.

    In the Scandinavian countries, the philosophy of "good design for everyday use," proposed by Sweden's Gregor Paulsson several decades earlier, informed the work of their celebrated first generation of furniture craftsmen. Pioneering Finn Alvar Aalto and Swede Bruno Mathsson were eclipsed by Danes such as Hans Wegner and Finn Juhl, who stirred up

Torso Armchair, Paolo Deganello (Italy)
1982
Leather, enamelled steel

Fifties-retro style blends with eighties comfort in a multifunctional design with curving back segments that move to envelop the occupant. Deganello, a leader in the Italian radical design movement, was a founder of Archizoom.

PK 12 Armchair, Poul Kjærholm (Denmark)
1962
Matte chrome-plated steel, leather

Departing from the familiar Scandinavian aesthetic of wood with a handcrafted look, this sleek design relates more closely to that of Bauhaus designers. In working with spare silhouettes and materials like steel and glass, Kjærholm was ahead of his time—and out of step with Danish designers.

Lounge Chair, Fabio Lenci (Italy)
1970
Glass, plastic, aluminum, leather

A comfort-minded version of see-through furniture from Italy, in an era when transparency was newly fashionable – the Italians and French had both introduced plastic blow-up chairs, introduced in Italy and France, were a novelty variant on the idea.

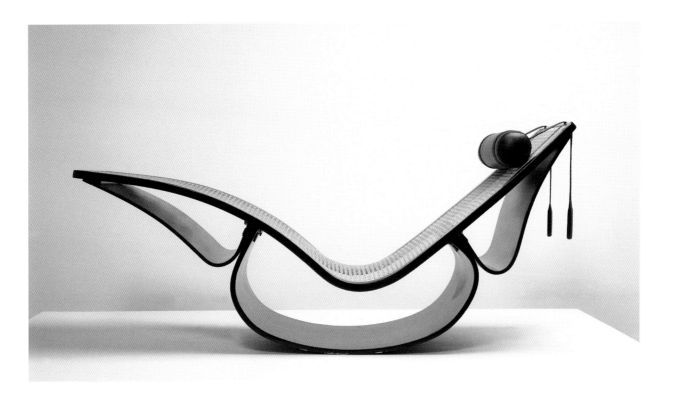

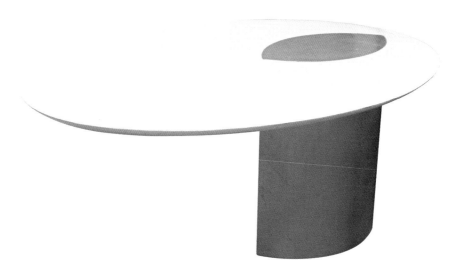

Rio Rocking Chaise Longue
Oscar Niemeyer (Brazil)
1978
Painted bentwood, caning, leather,
brass

Its reclining surface balanced on a
central bentwood curve, this chaise was
designed by the most famous Brazilian
architect of the twentieth century.
Niemeyer became internationally
celebrated for designing Brasilia,
the country's capital city.

Lunario Table, Cini Boeri (Italy)
1972
Formica top, aluminum base

Workaday materials treated luxuriously
in a one-of-a-kind design, a prototype.

the Scandinavian Modern fever that spread across most of the Western world and beyond.

Upstaging Nordic style, postwar designers and manufacturers in Italy, with Gio Ponti as tastemaker and *Domus* editor, broke with a tradition of modern interiors that embraced the past and produced objects with no context, often unglamorous materials, and unexpected shapes, which were a lively relief to hard-edged Modernism—and more attention-getting than the understated Scandinavian designs. Joe Colombo, Mario Bellini, and the Castiglioni brothers became, if not household names, certainly celebrities to the design cognoscenti. On its heels, the "counter-design" movement sought to escape materi-

alism in functional environments that saw the home as a reflection of—or perhaps a vehicle for—social and cultural change.

America's first important generation of modern designers, most famously Charles and Ray Eames, Eero Saarinen, Harry Bertoia, and their classmates at Cranbrook Academy—trained by expatriate Finn Eliel Saarinen—devised original new furniture forms, many of which employed newly developed materials and technology. Furniture of plywood and fiberglass, stacking chairs and occasional tables, flexible storage and multipurpose objects showed a down-to-earth con-

Bouloum Chair, Olivier Mourgue (France)
1969
Reinforced polyester, resin. Also in upholstered fiberglass

A modern translation of the traditional chaise into a witty anthropomorphic silhouette. Mourgue, like his countryman Pierre Paulin, designed seating with bold organic forms, experimenting with new types of construction. The Bouloum, named for a childhood friend, was in the Design Since 1945 exhibition and is in the collection of the Museum of Modern Art.

Minguren I Coffee Table,
George Nakashima (United States)
1981
Buckeye burl top, walnut base

As with all Nakashima works, the natural form of the wood slab determines the tabletop shape and ornamentation.

cern for practicality; flashy appearance was a lower priority. The Museum of Modern Art's Good Design exhibitions of 1950–55 showcased objects that would, as a brochure stated, "express the spirit of our times." These were simple forms of modern materials, clear in their purpose and generally unpretentious. Among them were Wegner's classic "the Chair"; Eero Saarinen's "Womb Chair"; designs by Marcel Breuer, Charles and Ray Eames, and Edward Wormley; and many everyday objects for household use. Less unconventional and more affordable than the sophisticated but far costlier furniture by Bauhaus masters, many of these objects would become icons of Midcentury Modern design. It should be noted, however, that the conservative nature of the Good Design objects was not so much a reflection of the designers' limitations as of marketing considerations: the exhibits were limited to objects that were actually in production and available to a relatively broad consumer market.

The focus on design excellence was not limited to American institutions. During the same decade as the MoMA Good Design exhibitions, several other countries—including Great Britain, Germany, Italy, and Japan—established organizations or annual award programs to recognize superior design in furniture and a variety of consumer goods.

In architecture, as the International Style gained ground, it was almost universally and rigorously applied in corporate construction. Its influence on residential architecture was subtler but equally profound. Open plans and the melding of interior and exterior spaces were requisites of the prototypical suburban home, making the results not so much individualistic as reconfigured to fit a middle-class mold—and as lacking in variety as the stark, steel-glass-and-leather, Bauhaus-style interiors.

Cobra Table Lamp, Angelo Lelli
(Italy)
1970
Brass, painted metal
A witty and provocative design
with an Italian accent.

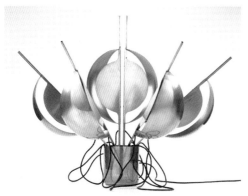

Ekstrem Chair, Terje Ekström
(Norway)
1972 (produced from 1984)
Fabric, polyurethane foam, metal
skeleton

The spidery shape, more comfortable
than it appears, has a flexible frame that
accommodates many seating postures.

Lamp, Jean-Perre Vitrac (France)
1970
Stainless steel

As much a piece of sculpture
as it is a lamp.

Crescent Rocker, Wendell Castle
(United States)
1975
Carved walnut, upholstery

Luna Lamp, Rinaldo Cutini (Italy)
1970
Stainless steel

Lockheed Lounge, Marc Newson (Australia)
1986
Fiberglass-reinforced polyester resin, blind-riveted
sheet aluminum, rubber-coated polyester resin

Probably the most published design of its time, this
limited-edition piece, recalling an eighteenth-century
French form, was named for a midcentury Boeing
aircraft that suggested the surface treatment. It was
shown in the exhibition European Design Since
1985: Shaping the New Century. Newson studied
jewelry design and sculpture, opening his London
office in 1997. In 2005, *Time* magazine named him
one of the world's 100 most influential people.

Cabinet with Two Doors, Wendell Castle
(United States)
ca. 1980
Quilted maple, partially painted
with ebonized finishes

DEFINING THE TRENDS, 1970-2000

The following sections define the major design directions of three decades, describing their most important characteristics and incorporating these in renderings of archetypal interiors.

Each movement is treated independently, accompanied by photographs of furnishings to illustrate the lively, overlapping, and sometimes confusing mix of styles that have, over these decades, marched under the banner of Modernism and carried its heritage into the twenty-first century.

The images are a broad and varied selection encompassing both the typical and the most innovative, most celebrated, and distinctive objects of their time. Though relatively recent in historic terms, many have already been deemed worthy of iconic status—acquired by museums and private collectors, traded by auction houses and dealers, and featured in design magazines, websites, and books. For more recent designs, no prognosis can be made. Many will fade into obscurity or be preserved as idiosyncratic artifacts of an era, but some will become touchstones for future generations. The jury is still out.

SCANDINAVIAN DESIGN

The Scandinavian Modern interior was an appealing alternative to the steel-and-glass Modernist style, with a fresh natural look and earth-tone color scheme. This room is typically understated and furnished with classic designs from Nordic masters: Alvar Aalto chairs at the counter, Arne Jacobsen chairs around the dining table, and Hans Wegner seats in the living area flanked by a Borge Mogensen sofa. The Verner Panton lighting and Gustavsberg ceramics are typical Scandinavian finishing touches—here with the unexpected surprise of a George Nelson ball clock.

RELAXING MODERNISM

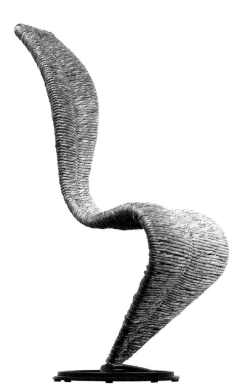

Even through the golden years of Midcentury Modernism, there ran a stubborn strain of resistance to abandoning the past. Historicist-oriented designers like Edward Wormley, Harvey Probber, and others encouraged a more inclusive aesthetic approach that brought several unrelated but equally influential movements to the surface by the 1970s. A slight change of

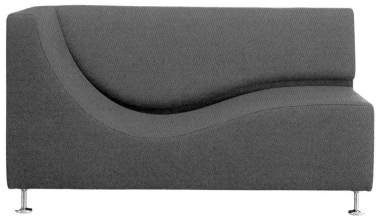

direction was signaled by the introduction of the term "Contemporary" in place of the more difficult "Modern." Though in part a semantic device, it signaled not so much a watering down as a freeing up: Modernism was being presented in less intimidating ways in order to mitigate its negative associations. There was a definite leaning toward more user-friendly and less rule-bound aesthetics, the most important of which were the Studio Craft movement and the renaissance of design in Italy.

S Chair, Tom Dixon (United Kingdom, b. Tunisia)
1991
Lacquered metal, woven marsh straw or wicker or fixed upholstery
Recalling the cantilevered form of Verner Panton's injection-molded plastic S stacking chair, this piece was shown in the exhibition European Design Since 1985: Shaping the New Century. Largely self-taught, Dixon has enjoyed a peripatetic career that has included graphic design, metal fabrication, manufacturing and retailing businesses, and designing furnishings and interiors. From 1998 to 2008 he was creative director for Habitat. His works are in the collections of leading design museums, and in 2001 he was awarded the Order of the British Empire.

Three Sofa de Luxe System
Jasper Morrison (United Kingdom)
1992
Plywood and multidensity polyurethane foam, die-cast polished aluminum, fabric or leather
A graduate of both Kingston Polytechnic and the Royal College of Art, Morrison has designed interiors, exhibitions, household products, and transportation systems as well as furniture.

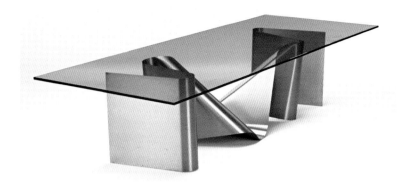

Table, François Monnet (France)
1970
Stainless steel, glass

Millepiede Table, Franco Campo
and Carlo Graffi (Italy)
ca. 1952/reintroduced 1975
Acero, glass, brass

Ellipse Tables, Guy de Rougemont
(France)
1970
Aluminum

Al Bombo, Stefano Giovannoni (Italy)
2002
Stainless steel, polished die-cast
aluminum

Bird Sofa, Michiel van der Kley
(Netherlands)
1999
Leather or fabric upholstery, polished
aluminum legs

A monolithic form whose shape
changes depending on the angle
of viewing.

Floating Seat and Back Sofa
Vladimir Kagan (United States,
b. Germany)
1970
Walnut, upholstery

A modern furniture designer who
refuses to abandon organic forms,
Kagan has championed a curvilinear
aesthetic in his distinctive seating
designs over more than half a century.

Architectural Variations

The tale of Modernism's transformation is most often told in terms of architecture, but its initial shifts were in variations of form rather than actual changes in direction. Architectural standard-bearer Philip Johnson and forward thinkers such as the "New York Five"—Charles Gwathmey, Richard Meier, Peter Eisenman, Michael Graves, and John Hejduk—sought to reenergize Modernism's sterile aesthetic, conceiving their structures almost as works of art. Buildings like Gwathmey Siegel's de Menil residence and the warm-colored homes of Rafael Moneo diverged from International Style formula, eliciting emotional as well as intellectual responses. In another departure, Louis Kahn and Paul Rudolph's innovative structures were perhaps too radical to garner broad popular appeal—and their unflattering designation as Brutalist didn't help. Nevertheless, in gradually varying iterations, the conception of Modernism was undergoing a reevaluation, morphing from its original inflexibility to something more fluid.

DESIGN AFTER MODERNISM

Woosh Sofa, Zaha Hadid (United Kingdom, b. Iraq)
1986
Upholstery, leather, lacquered fiberglass,
enameled and chrome-plated steel, Alcantara

Exaggerated, swooping curves are characteristic of the dynamic forms seen in Hadid's architecture. This early furniture design by Hadid is one of very few known examples. Her early avant-garde Deconstructivist designs exist only on paper; her first completed building was the Vitra fire station in 1994. In 2004 she became the first woman to be awarded the Pritzker Prize in architecture, and in 2006 the Guggenheim Museum mounted a retrospective exhibition of her work.

Hat Trick Chair and Ottoman
Frank Gehry (United States, b. Canada)
1992
Bent and woven maple laminate

An homage to handcraft, but also
indebted to Thonet, Aalto, and Eames.
The woven structure is springier than
bentwood, and the pattern of the seat
suggests basketry. From the Powerplay
Series of designs influenced by (and
named for) moves in ice hockey, in
honor of Gehry's favorite sport.

Saratoga Group, Lella and Massimo
Vignelli (United States, b. Italy)
1964
High-gloss polyester-lacquered wood,
leather upholstery, goose-down filling

The Italian aesthetic, dressed up for
American taste and marketed through
the innovative Stendig showroom, one
of the early U.S. importers of avant-
garde Italian design. The Vignellis,
husband and wife, design individually
and together—Massimo, a graphic
designer, created a landmark map for
the New York subway system.

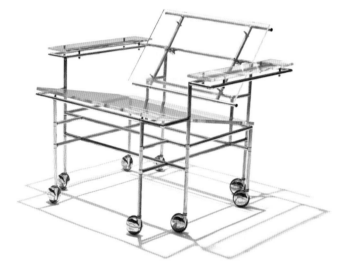

Nomos Dining Table
Norman Foster (United Kingdom)
1989
Powder-coated steel, glass, rubber

Rolling Lounge Chair, Paul Rudolph
(United States)
1968
Plexiglas, chrome-plated steel

Modern materials in a chair more
suggestive of architecture than of
furniture—logical, in view of Rudolph's
career as one of the most innovative
architects of the 1950s and 1960s. His
best-known works include the Art and
Architecture Building at Yale University,
where he was dean from 1958 to
1964, and his own 1961 New York
townhouse, with its interesting lucite
platforms and railingless walkways.

Queen Anne Side Chair
Robert Venturi (United States)
1985
Laminate over plywood

A visual quotation of a familiar form,
patterned with a tongue-in-cheek
"grandmother's tablecloth" design,
from a series of takeoffs on familiar
period chair styles.

Armchairs, Richard Meier
(United States)
1982
Lacquered wood

Furniture by a celebrated architect,
paying faint homage to Josef Hoffmann
and Charles Rennie Mackintosh though
updated with precise geometry and a
sleek lacquer finish. Featured in the
exhibition High Styles.

Pipistrello Lamp, Gae Aulenti (Italy)
1966
Steel, plastic

Featured in the exhibition Italy:
The New Domestic Landscape,
one of several innovative furniture
and lighting designs by a prominent
woman architect and one of the
pioneer Italian modernists. It is in
the collection of the Metropolitan
Museum of Art and others.

1970s

Relaxing the restrictions of orthodox Modernism, interiors in
the 1970s became less predictable and more personalized. In this
room, the newly fashionable conversation-pit area takes center
stage for companionable and comfortably cushioned seating.
Warren Platner chairs surround an Eero Saarinen table for dining, and the lighting is a multifaceted mix: recessed and concealed
illumination in the ceiling coffers, a Stilnovo chandelier, and an
Arredoluce lamp with a space-age look. A mirrored wall sets off
the mix of accessories.

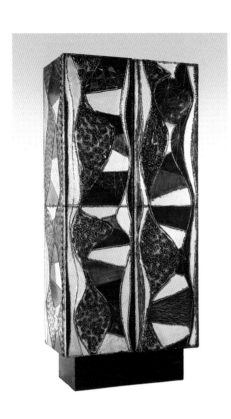

As interiors moved beyond the midcentury mode, they adopted a broader vocabulary of shape and color and a more open-minded attitude about accessorizing. In pursuit of personal style and individuality, designers embraced Americanized Scandinavian, revived Art Deco, and recaptured Colonial, suggesting a willingness to accept the past rather than escape it. Curves were introduced as either alternatives or counterpoints to strict linearity; interiors might be sculpted into ovals or circular spaces; floors were broken into multilevel sections; and platform seating created smaller, more intimate areas within open-plan rooms. The conversation pit, introduced by Eero Saarinen in 1957, was adopted and rearranged in almost endless variations. As the profession of interior design came into its own, designers—and their clients—pursued individuality, applying the lively colors, bold patterns, and sensual textures that had been disdained by International Style adherents. Pop-art patterned fabric and wallpaper, deeply textured or shag carpets, and accent area rugs proliferated. Concealed or track lighting set the mood, while mirrors and mirror-paneled screens, smoked glass, and sometimes even neon or disco-ball fixtures added glitter effects. Furniture might assume the organic forms of Vladimir Kagan seating or the macho-metal geometry of Paul Evans—polar opposites but equally removed from Bauhaus influences.

The casual look of the laid-back California Style was another manifestation of a style in transition, showcased in a series of thirteen exhibitions held between 1954 and 1976 at the Pasadena Art Museum that featured production and studio furniture as well as a variety of crafts and industrial design objects. It highlighted the creative talents of designers such as Paul Tuttle, Danny Ho Fung, Charles Hollis Jones, and the team of Hendrik Van Keppel and Taylor Green, as well as the relaxed approach of West Coast designers and producers.

Two-Door Cabinet with Biomorphic Forms
Paul Evans (United States)
1968
Wood, sculpted aluminum
This artisan-designer developed his own distinctive techniques of welding and sculpting metal; here, bold asymmetrical forms are sculpted in silver and black to create an intricately decorated surface. The design on each studio-made piece in this collection is slightly different. Evans's skilled metalwork reflects his training as a silversmith and sculptor.

Rocking Chair, Frank Gehry
(United States, b. Canada)
1970
Corrugated cardboard, masonite

Seeking a way to produce store fittings at a low cost, Gehry first developed the innovative Easy Edges collection in 1970. Functional, economical, and disposable, it was a novelty in its time but inspired succeeding applications of the quotidian material. Each element is cut separately and then assembled in a method of fabrication that enables both curves and angles; it was patented in 1978. Shown in the exhibition Design Since 1945.

Zocker Chair, Luigi Colani (Germany)
1973
Extruded plastic

DS 1025 Seating Units, Ubald Klug
(Switzerland)
1973
Wood, foam, leather

Individual terrace-shaped units can be used in pairs as shown or back-to-back, and may also be arranged into multiple-section modulars.

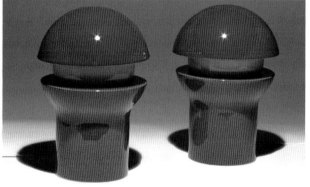 

Armchair, Jack Rogers Hopkins
(United States)
1972
Carved laminated birch

One of only five of its kind, each made
to order, this chair is closer to sculpture
than craft, and typical of Hopkins's
biomorphic forms. His work was
prominently featured in the California
Design 11 exhibition at the Pasadena
Art Museum in 1971.

Table Lamp, Timo Sarpaneva
(Finland)
1972
Porcelain, glass

Cloud Lamp, Ueli Berger (Germany)
1977
Plastic

1980s

The extravagant years of the 1980s were reflected in interiors furnished in grand gestures and a dressed-up style. The Vladimir Kagan–style overscaled sofa and Fabio Lenci Plexiglas-sided chairs shown here are typical of the era. A grand piano, on a stage-like platform and backed by a curving glass-block wall, might be as much for show as for playing music. The Ettore Sottsass ceiling lamp and recessed cove lighting cast an ambient glow on the ready-for-entertaining setting.

Cocoons and Comets

While most so-called Contemporary rooms reflected a surface change rather than substantial innovation, they did herald a new interest in creature comfort. This was in part the reflection of a popular-culture trend, the movement defined as "cocooning" by forecaster Faith Popcorn. Considering the home as a refuge from the stress of the modern world, it endorsed interiors with voluptuous seating, flannel upholstery, and "shabby chic" slipcovers. Later in the same quarter-century, the recession of the late 1980s closed out a decade of extravagance and acquisitiveness. It ushered in the "flea-market look" and a new appreciation of the simpler things in life—which might include anything from collections of vintage toys to needlepoint pillows

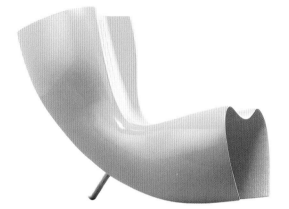

or travel mementos. In the movement toward more comfortable interiors, modulars and sectional sofas proliferated: overscaled, overstuffed pieces that provided capacious seating—and practically the only furniture necessary to fill a living room. Reflecting the interest in new materials that had begun in the postwar years, furniture of plastics or plywood was ubiquitous, often with colorful lacquer finishes. Plexiglas and Lucite tables were framed in chrome or brass, and accessories or ornament suggesting astronomical or rocket images reflected an infatuation with space exploration and the 1969 moon landing. The furniture introduced in the 1970s by fashion designer Pierre Cardin was futur-

Felt Chair, Marc Newson (Australia)
1989
Lacquered fiberglass, aluminum

One of Newson's familiar organic forms, which he made as seating pieces and tables in several different materials, including woven, aluminum, and fiberglass.

Sofa, Milo Baughman (United States)
c. 1975
Upholstery over wood frame

istic in form and disco-style in aesthetic, featuring glossy lacquer and polished plastic with metal fittings (London's Design Museum starred it in a 2000 exhibition).

Cardin was one of the first to capitalize on the possibilities of name-branded furniture, a vogue that has grown exponentially and continues to the present day. At around the same time, interior designer Angelo Donghia was the first to design (successfully) sheets and later (unsuccessfully) a collection of mass-market furniture. Calvin Klein and many others followed, introducing furnishings and household products that promised the comfort of association with a familiar

and accepted name rather than the riskier option of avant-garde style.

The last quarter-century was a stellar one for American design and designers in general, as architects moved into designing furnishings and objects—Frank Gehry, Richard Meier, Robert Venturi, Michael Graves, and Robert A. M. Stern among them—and artists like Scott Burton, Sol Le Witt, and Robert Wilson crossed over into the decorative arts.

Console, Charles Hollis Jones (United States)
c. 1975
Lucite, chrome-plated steel
In an era when acrylic furniture was all the rage, Jones became known for his sophisticated designs in this material. His work was featured in the California Design exhibitions at the Pasadena Art Museum.

Feltri Chair, Gaetano Pesce (Italy) 1987
Felt, polyester resin, rope
Soaked in polyester resin, the upholstery of the chair becomes its support structure—denser on the bottom for rigidity and lighter on the top, which adjusts like a collar to the user's taste. Published in Landmarks of 20th Century Design and featured in major museum collections.

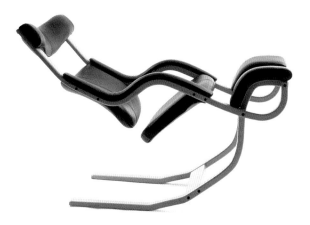

Bench for Two, Nanna Ditzel (Denmark)
1989
Laminated aircraft plywood, sycamore,
matte chrome, silver

A departure from the traditional techniques
of Danish cabinetmaking, these were fabricated with wood-bending technology used in
making aircraft. Ditzel was the most famous
woman in the first generation of Scandinavian designers, designing furniture with her
husband Jørgen until his death in 1961, and
later moving in more experimental directions
in furniture, jewelry, and textiles.

Paris Table, André Dubreuil (France)
1988
Flame-decorated and welded steel

Dubreuil is best known for his 1986 Spine
chair, but most of his work is in unique handcrafted furniture, ceramics, and lighting. This
table, with a skirtlike apron and leopardlike
spots, was made in an edition of twelve, with
an accompanying chair. The chair appeared
in the European Design Since 1985: Shaping
a New Century exhibition.

Gravity, Peter Opsvik (Norway)
1983
Beech, cherry, rosewood, fabric
or leather

A rocking variation of the
Balans kneeling chair—a concept
developed by Opsvik in 1979.

ITALIAN

Inventive Italian designers of the postwar era broke with convention to create furniture in bold new silhouettes and brighter colors that brought a fresh look to modern interiors. These new forms were complementary companions to an international mix of furniture and accessories. Here, the curvy shape of a multisectioned sofa by Ueli Berger, Eleanora Peduzzi-Riva, and Heinze Ulrich anchors the living area, facing off to Frenchman Guy de Rougemont aluminum coffee tables and a sleek stainless-steel bench. By the window is Joe Colombo's distinctive tube chair; and the bright yellow chandelier is a modern take on Venetian glass lighting.

The Italian Phenomenon

Italian postwar design surfaced toward the 1960s and became an international phenomenon in the decade that followed, producing some of the most innovative and appealing objects of the century. Rebuilding a war-ravaged industry, Italian designers used whatever resources were available to them, finding new and original ways to create attention-getting furniture and lighting that reflected both their skill at improvisation and their interest in machine-age technology. Most of the widely

celebrated designs of this era were introduced at the Triennale exhibitions in Milan, which had begun in 1923 in Monza, Italy, and relocated to Milan in 1933. The exhibitions had drawn attention outside the sponsoring country, but from 1951 (the first full-scale postwar event) the Triennale became the most influential international showcase for new design.

To bring their unconventional ideas to fruition, Italian designers had supportive partners: small manufacturers seeking to rebuild their businesses, geared to small production runs, and willing to take chances on untried concepts. Together they turned out a fertile stream of original objects—modular

Golem SD 51, Vico Magistretti (Italy)
ca. 1970s
Lacquered wood, leather seat

Soriana Sofa, Afra and Tobia Scarpa (Italy)
1970
Leather, foam, chrome-plated steel
Low-sitting tufted leather forms were among the celebrated Italian seating concepts of the postwar Modern era. This design, distinctive for the external metal frame that supports its foam cushioning, was by a celebrated husband-and-wife architectural team, whose designs were featured in the *Italy: The New Domestic Landscape* and *Design Since 1945* exhibitions, and are in many museum collections.

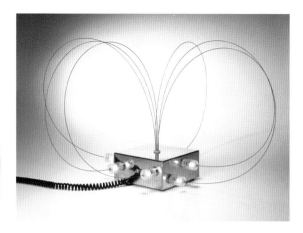

DESIGN AFTER MODERNISM

Lips Sofa, Studio 65 (Italy)
1971
Wool over polyurethane

An homage to an infamous Mae West sofa designed by artist Salvador Dalí in 1935, this adventurous object, dubbed "Marilyn" for actress Marilyn Monroe, became a standard-bearer of the Italian design explosion and was shown in Italy: The New Domestic Landscape exhibition.

Piumino Sofa, Jonathan de Pas, Donato D'Urbino, and Paolo Lomazzi (Italy)
1970
Leather, foam, wood

Table Lamp, Arditi and Gianni Gamberini (Italy)
1971
Chrome-plated steel, wire, magnet, lacquered wood

Cab Armchairs, Mario Bellini (Italy)
1977
Flexible steel, saddle leather

A steel skeleton is wrapped in a skin of fine Italian leather, zipped like the covers of upholstered furniture. The chair was included in the Design Since 1945 exhibition. Its designer, editor of the magazine Domus from 1986 to 1991, was given a retrospective exhibition at the Museum of Modern Art in 1987.

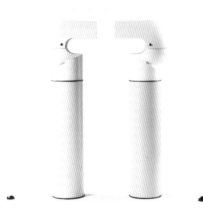

sofas in bold, sweeping forms or fat-cushioned geometrics, tables and seating shells of colorful injection-molded plastic, lots of leather, and a plentiful helping of humor. Form rather than function was primary in furniture that nonetheless functioned perfectly well, often in multipurpose designs, and was witty or topical into the bargain. The designs included a lip-shaped sofa, a plastic blow-up chair, and another shaped like a baseball glove; these and other traffic-stopping pieces made the unfamiliar point that furniture could be fun. For lighting, the Italians fomented a revolution in a moribund field, bringing new life to the category, inventing applications for recently developed halogen bulbs, and offering the first true departures from conventional lamps and fixtures. As decorative as they were efficient, they were ideal companions to modern furniture. Their innovative forms were endlessly copied—and still are.

Interiors furnished with the new Italian designs were extroverted, informal, and unabashed in their applications of bright color and bold accents. In contrast to so-called Contemporary spaces, they were anything but understated; though respectful of the Modernist idiom, they ignored its restrictions, refusing to take themselves, or design, too seriously. Joe Colombo, Mario Bellini, Gaetano Pesce, Achille and Pierluigi Castiglioni, and Gae Aulenti were among the most celebrated of the Italians who laid the groundwork for the more radical Postmodern movement. MoMA's 1972 exhibition Italy: The New Domestic Landscape introduced now-classic designs from many of these designers to a broader audience, and their enthusiastic—if somewhat taken aback—response helped to encourage adventurous explorations in design beyond Italy.

Joe Chair, Jonathan de Pas, Donato D'Urbino, and Paolo Lomazzi (Italy)
1970
Leather over metal frame and polyurethane foam, casters

This archetype of the Postmodern concept of furniture as symbol—a giant catcher's mitt named for Italian designer Joe Colombo (though many sources credit baseball star Joe DiMaggio as the inspiration) was shown in the exhibitions Italy: The New Domestic Landscape and Design Since 1945.

Floor Lamps, Gae Aulenti (Italy)
1975
Plastic, chrome-plated steel

Proust Armchair, Alessandro Mendini
(Italy)
1978
Handpainted and carved wood, painted
fixed fabric

An exaggerated Victorian form (named for
the writer who might have sat in it), designed
when Mendini was a member of Studio
Alchimia, and perhaps the best-known
example of Radical Design's mockery
of classic forms and standards of taste.
The impressionist upholstery pattern was
handpainted. In the collection of the Metropolitan Museum of Art, among many others.

Table Lamp, Gino Sarfatti (Italy)
1966
Enameled steel, leather

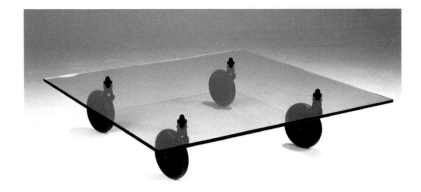

Table Lamp, Arredoluce (Italy)
1970
Enameled and chrome-plated steel, marble

Sansonel Table, Gaetano Pesce (Italy)
1980
Molded polyester resin

In his decades-long career, Pesce moved
beyond Arte Povera—the late 1960s anti-
establishment movement that embraced the
use of everyday materials—to experiments in
foam or plastics: materials that are flexible and
sometimes unpredictable, as in this random-
shaped table, which varies with each iteration.

Tavolo Con Ruote Coffee Table
Gae Aulenti (Italy)
1980
Plate glass, metal, casters

Industrial casters, in place of legs,
are secured with metal brackets to a
plate-glass top, less than one foot off
the floor, in a design that has become
an icon of industrial-chic style and the
most famous work by this member of
the Italian avant-garde.

Modular Seating Units, Luigi Colani
(Germany)
1970
Upholstery over foam, plastic, rubber

Seating sectionals like this heralded a
more casual approach to interior furnishings, reflecting the informal lifestyle
of the era—though most were not so
close to the floor.

STUDIO CRAFT

Interiors influenced by the Studio Craft movement embraced the warmth
of textured wood and stone, handwoven textiles, and handcrafted furniture.
This interior, with its cathedral-like ceiling, suggests a vernacular structure in
its use of natural materials. On one side of the old-fashioned fireplace-cooking
island are a George Nakashima dining table and chairs; on the other are
a simple settee, wood coffee table, and artisanal slat-back rocking chair.
An Isamu Noguchi Akari lamp, handcrafted ceramics, and handwoven rugs
on a flagstone floor add the finishing touches.

Studio Craft

The Studio Craft movement emerged in the 1960s as a response to the impersonality of machine-made furniture and standardized production. Craft had been marginalized by industrialization, but rather than campaigning against mechanization, late-twentieth-century craftsmen took a more rational approach, using technology where it suited their needs but focusing on handwork to forge a parallel path to the marketplace.

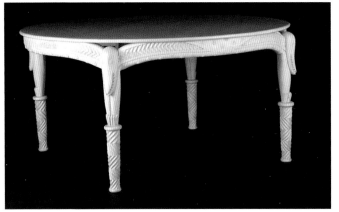

The new craft culture was largely an American phenomenon, nurtured by artisans working individually or with a few assistants in studios or workshops, and developed into a full-scale movement that gained respect for its practitioners and has continued to the present day, thriving in the areas of ceramics, glass, metalwork, textiles, basketry, even paper, as well as wood. Craftsmen viewed their furniture and objects as personal creations rather than production items, and followed no specific style. The traditional apprentice system was gradually supplanted by more formal training, from single-focus schools and workshops to sophisticated college arts programs

Music Stand on Three Legs
Wharton Esherick (United States)
1962
Carved cherry

Considered the "dean of American craftsmen," Esherick studied art and began his career as a painter but began sculpting wood in the 1920s, progressing from Arts & Crafts angular forms to the curvilinear shapes that made him famous. An Esherick music stand was included in The Maker's Hand: American Studio Furniture, 1940–1990 at the Museum of Fine Arts Boston in 2003, and another is in the collection of the Metropolitan Museum of Art.

Dining Table, Judy Kensley McKie
(United States)
1986
Maple

An important figure in the Studio Craft movement, McKie studied painting at the Rhode Island School of Design, but as a woodworker she is self-trained. She is known for the frequent use of animal forms in her sculptural furniture, and her work has been included in exhibitions at the Museum of Fine Arts Boston, the Museum of Arts and Design, and other venues. In 2005 the Furniture Society gave her its Award of Distinction.

that trained practitioners in any of the major crafts—though there remain those individuals who hone their skills independently. For all of them, local and national craft associations, trade shows, galleries, and museums were established to provide support systems, promotion, and exposure of their work. Many of these artisans continued to use centuries-old techniques—carving, inlay and marquetry, molding, lacquerwork, and more—but they were joined by many others who have broken new ground, using unconventional objects, man-made materials, and techniques of their own devising.

In 1957, the Museum of Contemporary Crafts (now the

Museum of Arts and Design) in New York introduced Wharton Esherick, Sam Maloof, Tage Frid, George Nakashima, and other first-generation studio craftsmen to the general public. By the 1970s designer-craftsmen such as Wendell Castle, Jere Osgood, and Arthur Espenet Carpenter were establishing their reputations by making objects that showed not only artistic excellence but also sophisticated cabinetry and precision woodworking skills. Increasingly skilled in marketing techniques, they and others like them began to gain both exposure and prestige, elevating themselves and their work to a status equaling that of other creative professionals.

Rocking Chaise Lounge
Michael Hurwitz (United States)
1989
Painted bentwood mahogany

Made for the 1989 New Handmade Furniture exhibition at the Museum of Fine Arts Boston. Trained in Boston University's Program in Artisanry, Hurwitz follows in the tradition of earlier studio craftsmen, exhibiting his work in both museums and galleries.

Rocker, Sam Maloof (United States)
1969
Walnut, ebony

A trademark design by a first-generation American studio craftsman. Each piece was made to individual order: Presidents Carter and Reagan owned Maloof rockers. In 1985 Maloof was the first craftsman to receive a MacArthur "Genius" grant. A Maloof rocker was featured in the exhibition High Style, and in the Craft in America PBS series and traveling exhibition that opened at the Arkansas Art Center in 2007.

The forms of studio craft furniture differ according to the character of the materials used. Though the craftsman may produce many variations of a single design—even sometimes using machinery to form or finish them—each piece is made individually and is therefore different and more personal than a machine-made object. With no prescribed style parameters, this category is defined entirely by the means of fabrication. Some objects are handmade versions of classic forms, some are inspired by vernacular objects, while still others are entirely the products of a fertile imagination. In contrast to designs produced by the more radical movements, most craft furni-

Console Table, Thomas Hucker
(United States)
1994
Pau ferro and wenge woods,
anodized aluminum, steel, waxed
linen lashing

Conoid Dining Table
George Nakashima (United States)
c. 1970s
Oak burl, walnut, rosewood

The conical form was inspired by the
cone-shaped roof of the designer's
studio. The form of the table is
determined by the shape of the original
wood slab, with rosewood "butterfly"
joints the only ornament. Nakashima,
perhaps the best known of all American
woodcrafters, had his studio and
production facility in New Hope, Penn-
sylvania. He learned his craft from a
Japanese carpenter while interned with
his family as enemy aliens during the
Second World War.

ture coexists comfortably with production pieces in interiors and dictates no particular design scheme. The makers themselves, taking different approaches to shaping and finishing the materials, form a bridge from historic artisanry to current and future design. In their search for expressive forms, the furniture of the studio craftsmen prefigured the design/art objects of the twenty-first century. Even the most historically influenced among them lie within the boundaries of a redefined Modernism.

Two Seater, Wendell Castle
(United States)
1977
Stack cherry laminate

Castle's wood pieces are instantly recognizable for their organic forms and the unique stack-laminating technique he developed—reflecting his training as a sculptor rather than a furniture maker. One of these is in the collection of the Metropolitan Museum of Art.

Conoid Bench, George Nakashima
(United States)
1971
Walnut

The free-form slab seat and spindle back are hallmarks of Nakashima's style, as is the distinctive overhang that creates a cantilever effect. One of these benches was shown in Objects: USA, the landmark survey of American studio crafts.

Serpent Side Table, Judy Kensley
McKie (United States)
c. 1980
Milk-painted wood and glass

Nature inspires the sinuous limbs
of a finely crafted unique piece.

Table, Albert Paley (United States)
1982
Forged and fabricated steel, slate

Stack Laminate Dining Table
Wendell Castle (United States)
1979
Laminated cherry wood

This is the largest work ever made using
the artist's trademark stack-laminated
technique.

Lamps, Richard Etts (United States)
1972
Plaster with enameled ivory finish

POSTMODERN

Less assertive than some of its architectural manifestations, the Postmodern-influenced interior celebrated vibrant color and pattern, rejecting International Style sameness but stopping short of kitsch. Here, a bright turquoise wall is a counterpoint to apple-green sofa and chairs. In the dining area, Robert Venturi's Queen Anne chairs in grandmother's-tablecloth laminate poke fun at traditional style. The unconventional shapes of a Memphis-style sofa and sideboard are set off against a zigzag-pattern wall, with more Memphis touches in the quirky accessories and lighting fixtures.

REJECTING MODERNISM

Postmodernism

Modernism had long been criticized for its severe and unyielding aesthetic. But Postmodernism attacked it on more serious grounds: its failure to connect with the public it professed to serve. The movement had its philosophical origins in the writings of Jacques Derrida and Michel Foucault, which disputed the idea that a single set of principles could apply to all circum-

stances, for all individuals. Less subversive than its intellectual roots, Postmodernism in design was manifested primarily in architecture and in America. Although Harvard architecture dean Joseph Hudnut had used the term as early as 1945, the movement emerged two decades later, largely instigated by Robert Venturi's books. It gained influential international advocates, including Aldo Rossi, Hans Hollein, Philippe Starck, and Arata Isozaki as well as Americans Michael Graves, Charles Moore, and Robert A. M. Stern. Reversing the doctrine of form following function, it put form in first place, though there was more to its aesthetic than simple visual impact.

Prince Chair, Mario Botta
(Switzerland)
1985
Enameled mesh steel, leather

Botta's furniture design echoes the strong geometric shapes of his architecture and an aesthetic that shares many of the qualities seen in designs from the Bauhaus. However, his work is more clearly Postmodernist—most notably, his much-published design for the San Francisco Museum of Modern Art, which opened in 1995.

Capitello Lounge Chair, Studio 65
(Italy)
1971
Polyurethane foam

Featured in Italy: The New Domestic Landscape, this is both a cheeky sendup of classicism and a functional seating piece. Self-contradictory, the form and the white finish suggest marble, but it is comfortably soft to sit on. It foretells the Postmodernist use of historic motifs, and has itself become something of a classic.

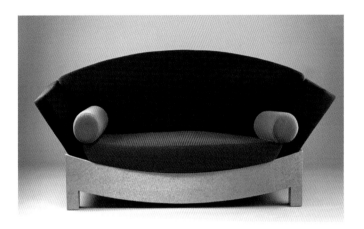

How High the Moon, Shiro Kuramata (Japan)
1986
Epoxy-coated nickel-plated steel

The silhouette of a soft upholstered armchair executed unexpectedly in metal, with an open weave that creates an airy look. Made in an edition of thirty and named for a Duke Ellington song, it is considered a landmark of twentieth-century design. One of the most innovative designers in postwar Japan, Kuramata conceived witty designs that melded Eastern simplicity and Western popular culture. He was an original member of the Memphis collective in Italy.

Mitzi Sofa, Hans Hollein (Austria)
1981
Wooden frame with veneer, polyurethane upholstery

Though he designed several pieces of furniture for the Memphis group, Hollein's most important work was in architecture. In 1985 he was awarded the prestigious Pritzker Prize.

Sheraton Chair, Robert Venturi (United States)
1986
Laminated plywood, screen-printed laminate, leather

Following the Postmodernist message of "double-coding," this chair takes the silhouette of an eighteenth-century classic for a machine-fabricated piece.

Postmodernism sought to return meaning to architecture by incorporating elements drawn from history and popular culture, elements that ordinary people could understand. Charles Jencks, in *What is Post-modernism?*, called this double-coding or multivalent messages.

At the peak of the movement's relatively short life—which didn't outlast the 1980s—Las Vegas and Los Angeles trumped Rome and Florence as sources of inspiration, in buildings that revived historical references with wit and irony and provided a multilayered experience that could evoke an emotional response, even from the architecturally unsophisti-

cated. Classical motifs were chopped up and often distorted in convention-flouting silhouettes, sparked with occasional notes of baroque or rococo. The assertive forms and fanciful colors of Postmodernism were a wholesale rejection of International Style architecture. Less radical in translating Postmodern concepts into residential buildings, architects grafted Palladian details onto shingle or clapboard-sided homes in suburban or seaside developments. In mixing past and present with abandon, the boldest Postmodern buildings were an exuberant chal-

First Chair, Michele De Lucchi (Italy)
1983
Plastic, painted steel, painted wood, rubber
One of the iconic Memphis designs, by one of its original members.

Tramonto a New York Sofa
Gaetano Pesce (Italy)
1980
Upholstery over foam
Paying homage to the metropolis, his home since 1980, Pesce shaped an unconventional sofa suggesting the city skyline at sunset, for a witty work that is as much performance piece as design object and has been showcased in many publications as well as in museum collections.

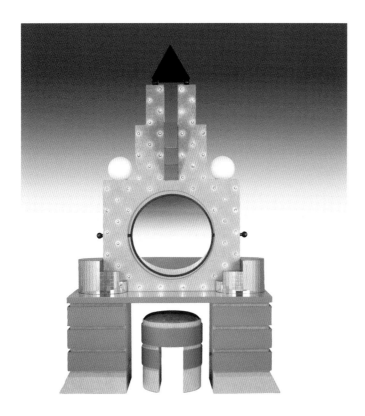

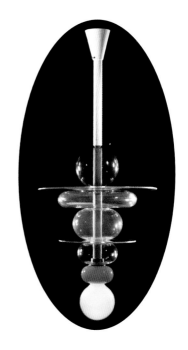

lenge to accepted standards of good design, sometimes going to awkward extremes in their rebellion against the status quo.

The new wave of the Italian avant-garde dominated Postmodern design. Although counterculture groups like Archigram (London, 1961), Archizoom and Superstudio (both founded in Florence, 1966), and Studio Alchimia (Milan, 1976) presaged the revolution to come, the iconic Postmodern objects in furniture, lighting, and accessories were conceived by Memphis, the infamous Italian collaborative that debuted at Milan's Salone Internazionale del Mobile in 1981 and was founded by architect and designer Ettore Sottsass.

Plaza Dressing Table and Stool
Michael Graves/Memphis (Italy)
1981
Maple root with enameled teal finish, mirror and mirrored pedestals, low-voltage bulbs, upholstery

Tweaking a traditional item of boudoir furniture, this Postmodern design is informed by both Biedermeier and Neoclassical styles. Graves, one of the major American architects linked to the Postmodern movement, has designed a number of witty household and kitchen accessories in the genre.

Firenze Chandelier, Ettore Sottsass
(Italy)
1995
Glass

Extroverted color in glass from the founder of Memphis, still in his Postmodern mode.

Its members included Alessandro Mendini, Andrea Branzi, Matteo Thun, and Michele de Lucchi, and later Shiro Kuramata, Michael Graves, Arato Isozaki, and Hans Hollein. Unquestionably different from anything then available, the furniture self-consciously replicated elements of recognizable architectural styles, using bright colors and laminates in provocative forms that ignored all preconceptions of good taste and often tossed functionalism aside. It was meant for shock value as much as for use—and to poke fun at more conventional objects. Having made its statement with considerable skill, and a proliferation of international media attention, Memphis disbanded in 1988.

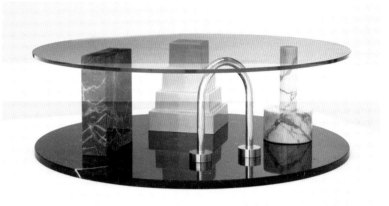

Postmodernism did not translate comfortably into interiors, since the designs were often impractical and visually disruptive in a room with other furniture. But it produced some notable works, including Ettore Sottsass's iconic bookshelves and Robert Venturi's laminated-and-lacquered plywood chairs parodying eighteenth- and nineteenth-century period styles. Postmodern design reached the broadest consumer market in decorative accessories like vases, candlesticks, and tableware that ranged from charming to kitschy. Despite their limitations, however, the designs of the Postmodern movement never failed to draw attention. In highly visible structures such as hotels

Wink Chair, Toshiyuki Kita (Japan)
1980
CFC-free polyurethane foam, polyester padding, tubular steel
Featured in the Design Since 1945 exhibition and in major museum collections, the articulated form of this whimsical seat is practical: it can be upright as a chair or recline as a chaise; the Mickey Mouse–like "ears" adjust forward or back; and the zippered covers remove for washing.

Park Coffee Table, Ettore Sottsass
(Italy)
1983
Glass, metal, stone, black marble

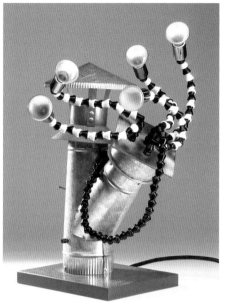

and public buildings, they encouraged a revival of interest in classical and traditional design. The movement's inclusive aesthetic, embracing many styles and aspects, mirrored the changing society that would bring a globalized market and equality for ethnic and gender minorities, and it is more significant in retrospect than when it was actually happening.

Bench, Andrea Branzi (Italy)
1985
Painted MDF, tree branches
A unique work from a series titled "Domestic Animals," by one of the founders of the Florence group Archizoom Association, and the founder of Domus Academy, the first international postgraduate school of design in Milan.

A Nite on Lindquist Ridge Table Lamp, Garry Knox Bennett (United States)
1990
Known for furniture that is as witty as it is well made, Bennett is an artist-craftsman whose work was given a 2001 retrospective at the American Craft Museum (now the Museum of Arts and Design). He is one of the first generation of trained practitioners—at the California College of the Arts—and his work is in many museum collections.

Carlton Bookshelf, Ettore Sottsass
(Italy)
1981
Wood, polychrome, and printed
laminate

One of the most familiar images from
the Memphis group, with a jagged
shape and clashing colors in quotidian materials—a blatant rejection of
conventional forms and dictates of good
design. Seen in the exhibition European
Design Since 1985: Shaping the New
Century and in many major museum
collections.

Pratfall Chair, Philippe Starck (France)
1982
Laminated mahogany-veneered wood,
painted tubular steel, leather

A larger version of a chair originally
made for Paris's Café Costes, designed
with only three legs to provide fewer
tripping hazards for waiters. Seen in the
exhibition European Design Since 1985:
Shaping the New Century. Both an
industrial and interior designer as well,
Starck is known for his witty household
objects and unconventional hotel
designs, including the Doral in Miami
and the Paramount in New York.

Deconstructivism

A similarly rebellious but more nihilistic style developing close on the heels of Postmodernism, Deconstructivism took another direction and produced fragmented architecture with jarring asymmetry. It was exemplified by structures like Frank Gehry's Santa Monica home (1978), Bernard Tschumi's Parc de la Villette (1984–87), and Peter Eisenman's Wexner Center for the Arts (1989) as well as the early works of architects like Rem Koolhaas, Zaha Hadid, Daniel Libeskind, Coop Himmelb(l)au, and James Wines. Many of their designs, too challenging and difficult for potential occupants to visualize, were never built and became influential primarily through striking renderings and models shown in museum exhibitions such as the 1988 Museum of Modern Art show Deconstructivist Architecture or in architectural and design publications. Deconstructivist buildings discarded conventional structural elements, breaking them apart to create jagged, irregular silhouettes with complex geometry that were striking anachronisms in the language of architectural forms. Adopting aspects of cubism and Russian constructivism, these architects rejected the historical references and ornament of Postmodernism. Like Postmodernism, however, the style was short-lived—though both were influential in emancipating designers from the structures of Modernism and expanding the visual vocabulary of modern design.

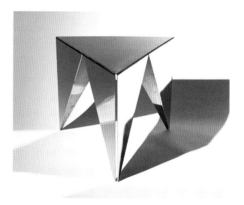

Pylon Chair, Tom Dixon
(United Kingdom)
1992
Enameled steel

Deceptively insubstantial in appearance, the intricate openwork wire form is made of individual rods, welded together by hand. The wing-sided high back is a final fillip on a chair that looks more like architectural framework than furniture.

Hectapod Table, Scott Burton
(United States)
1982
Folded nickel-plated steel

Prefiguring the design/art objects of the twenty-first century, Burton's work is in many museum collections as both art and furniture. The table is in a limited edition of six.

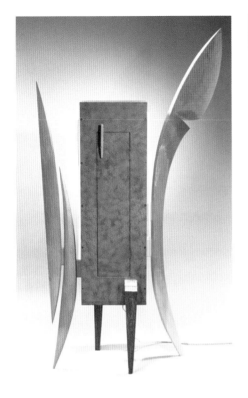

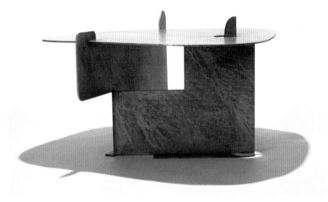

Cabinet, Wendy Maruyama
(United States)
1984
Polychrome, laminate, and neon

California-based, as were most of the
early Studio Craft artists, Maruyama
began making furniture in the 1970s.
Her work has been seen in *Breaking
Barriers: Recent American Craft* at
the American Craft Museum and in
the *Craft in America* PBS show and
traveling exhibition.

Scivolando Chair
Alessandro Mendini (Italy)
1983
Mirrored glass, wood

Prefiguring the design/art of the twenty-
first century, an "unsittable" seat from
a member of the avant-garde Studio
Alchimia.

Pierced Table (IN-82-2090)
Isamu Noguchi (United States)
1982
Hot-dipped galvanized steel

One of the few furniture designs
by this sculptor, made in a limited
edition of eighteen.

HIGH TECH

Urban lofts designed in the High Tech style made the most of turn-of-the-century factory buildings, restoring and refurbishing original wood floors, brick walls, and tin ceilings to create an entirely new type of living space. Here, furnishings are suitably simple: architect's drafting-table chairs for dining, factory-type stools at the counter, and basic Knoll sofa and chairs in the living area. Industrial-style shelving and a pegboard for pot storage are similarly unpretentious and efficient. The loft lighting combines bare-bulb fixtures, an industrial chandelier, and halogen lights strung on cables.

High Tech

A less intellectual approach, and therefore a less restrictive one, characterized the style labeled High Tech, after the 1978 book by Joan Kron and Suzanne Slesin in which the authors adopted the cutting-edge term to refer to architecture made with pre-fabricated elements and applied it to describe a movement in interior design. The book itself was actually a sourcebook of industrial products that could be used in residential spaces. Responding to the infatuation of Modernism with industrial

materials and technology, High Tech took the accoutrements of factory materials like glass blocks, tin ceilings, exposed wood beams, matte-finish metals, and lights strung on visible cables. Low platform seating, industrial carpeting, and factory shelving were dominant furnishings in these casual and clutter-free environments, with metal bowls and vases or glass laboratory containers as decorative accents. Thumbing its nose at elegance, High Tech substituted trendiness and a youthful attitude that was urban-based and media-friendly. The style came to characterize a new genre of residence—the loft—which began with

Floor Lamp, Arredoluce (Italy)
1970
Enameled and chrome-plated steel,
marble

Teatro, Marc Berthier (France)
1979
Solid beech, tempered glass
or in painted MDF

DEFINING THE TRENDS, 1970–2000

converted artists' studios in New York's SoHo neighborhood and ultimately spread to urban and suburban areas in new construction that mimicked the renovated industrial spaces of the originals. High Tech did not, for the most part, stimulate new furniture designs; rather, it adapted existing industrial forms for residential interiors. And its more austere variations generated the ascetic designs of Minimalism.

Coffee Table, Sol LeWitt
(United States)
1981
Lacquered wood, glass

Made in a limited edition of thirty pieces, this form has the spare geometry of sculptures by an artist considered one of the founders of Minimalism. LeWitt's serial sculptures and wall drawings played with both linearity and geometry, and an entire building devoted to his wall drawings opened at the Massachusetts Museum of Contemporary Art in 2008.

Fiche Male Lamp, Yonel Lebovici
(France)
1978
Aluminum, chrome-plated steel

Collapsible Table
Niels Jørgen Haugesen (Denmark)
1984
Ash, steel

A second-generation Danish modernist updates the traditional drop-leaf dining table.

Solomon Chair, Danny Lane
(United Kingdom, b. United States)
ca. 1988
Glass, steel

Disconcertingly fractured and stacked
for a statement that at once reflects and
rejects a conventional form, this is a
trademark work by the lone American
in London's 1980s avant-garde. The
rough combination of industrial materials and craft techniques was typical of
young designers' rebellion against strict
Modernism.

Etruscan Chair, Danny Lane
(United Kingdom, b. United States)
ca. 1984
Glass, stainless steel, and duralumin

The "fractured" edges of the glass, and
the skinny metal legs, suggest an archae-
ological find—a rejection of industrial
production. Shown in the exhibition
European Design Since 1985: Shaping
the New Century.

Avant-Garde Furniture

As architecture moved away from strict Modernism, so did furniture designers. The latter decades of the twentieth century saw them striking out in new directions, creating objects that could not be labeled as belonging to a single movement or

a particular style. The diversions from conventional forms took place in several countries. Verner Panton in Denmark and Eero Aarnio in Finland were among those whose furniture helped to reenergize Scandinavian design. In France, modernists Pierre Paulin and Olivier Mourgue broke with the French tradition of fine finishes and traditional shapes, and Maria Pergay and François Monnet were among those exploring new applications for industrial stainless steel by using it in furniture. The precedent-flouting partnerships of Elizabeth Garouste and Matteo Bonetti, and Claude and François-Xavier Lalanne,

Rover Chair, Ron Arad
(United Kingdom, b. Israel)
1981
Enameled steel, leather

A seat from a Rover automobile set on a frame of vintage scaffolding was the first work of "ready-made" furniture by Arad, then one of the rebellious young designers in 1980s London who combined industrial materials and handcraft techniques in pieces that challenged established design standards. The Rover was shown in the exhibition European Design Since 1945: Shaping the New Century and was featured in the MoMA's 2009 Arad retrospective.

Rex Armchair, Mats Theselius
(Sweden)
1995
Enameled steel, cherry, leather

A limited-edition piece, also made in a production version. Shown in the exhibition European Design Since 1985: Shaping the New Century. Theselius is one of the new avant-garde in Sweden, designing furniture focused more on concept than on current fashion.

Barbare Chair, Elizabeth Garouste
and Mattia Bonetti (France)
1981
Patinated bronze, hide, leather

These artists designed furniture of
sculpted metal with rough finishes and
an edgy, exotic aggressiveness that
reflected the rebellion against doctrinaire Modernism during the 1980s.
This chair, as with all of their designs,
was a limited edition.

Baby Balzac, Forrest Myers
(United States)
1991
Anodized aluminum wire

Furniture is a starting point rather than
the ultimate objective of the distinctive
woven wire seating units by this sculptor, one of the artists who showed at
the groundbreaking New York gallery
Art et Industrie in the 1980s. His 1974
work *The Wall* is a signature SoHo
landmark that serves as a gateway to
this New York neighborhood.

designed furniture and objects that were unconventional, original, and impossible to categorize. London erupted in the 1980s as a center of avant-garde design, with Tom Dixon, Danny Lane, Nigel Coates, and current superstars Israeli-born Ron Arad and Australian Marc Newson producing a new genre of studio furniture that challenged establishment

standards. Most of them played with industrial materials, sometimes recycling them and applying unexpected handcraft techniques in pieces that would anticipate the directions of twenty-first-century design. In America, the Greenwich Village gallery Art et Industrie showed designs that were something between furniture and art, including works by artists such as Forrest Myers and Michele Oka-Doner. Architect Frank Gehry played with corrugated cardboard; craftsmen began their crossover into art with Albert Paley's abstract metalwork and Wendell Castle and Alphonse Mattia's witty plastic creations; and artists such as Scott Burton and Donald Judd

Chest of Drawers, Tejo Remy
(Netherlands)
1991
Wood drawers, plastic, contact paper, paint, jute

Produced in an edition of 200 pieces, using found drawers from old chests glued to plywood frames and wrapped with movers' belting. The various components are stacked and belted by the users, making each iteration unique. Seen in the exhibition European Design Since 1985: Shaping the New Century. Remy's works are owned by major

museums including the Museum of Modern Art, the High Museum of Art, and London's Design Museum.

Miniature Angel Chair
Wendell Castle (United States)
1991
Bronze with verdigris patina

A divergence into metal by an artist best known for his work in wood.

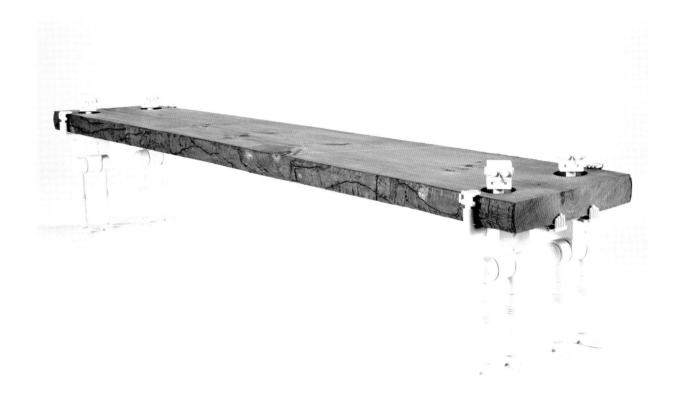

moved in the opposite direction with what was then called sculpture-furniture. More conceptual than visually inspired, most of the avant-garde designs were made unique or in limited numbers, and a number of them seem more like works-in-progress than finished pieces. But they were steps along a new path.

By the close of the century, design innovation had become international—with Italians, a new French avant-garde, icono-clastic Londoners, and a group of German Postmodernists. Off the European continent, a new generation of Swedes and Finns embraced "anti-design," a movement born in Italy in the 1960s,

White Pine Harvest Bench
Edward Zucca (United States)
1998
White pine, faux bark modeled in resin, and painted hard maple

Craft meets whimsy: resin is modeled to suggest natural bark, and painted robot figures with rotating heads replace conventional table legs. Zucca's work, most of natural hardwoods, uses other materials to complement the wood and to help express the visual narrative of his work.

rejecting the styles of their predecessors in favor of more provocative, often politically inspired design. And in Japan, the concept of "*kansei*," concerned with art that stimulated emotional as well as visual responses, produced designs that focused on elements like texture and softness. Most influential, and

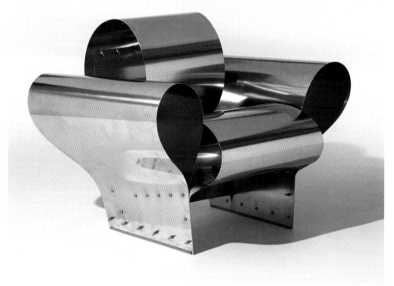

perhaps the indirect heirs to the Memphis tradition, were the Dutch designers at Droog—the design collaborative founded in Amsterdam in 1993 by Gijs Bakker and Renny Ramakers. At the crest of the avant-garde wave, they would become front-runners in the ranks of principled, free-thinking, and barrier-breaking creators who gave new life and meaning to the term Modernism in the early years of the twenty-first century.

Well Tempered Chair, Ron Arad
(United Kingdom, b. Israel)
1986
Tempered stainless steel, wing nuts

Hard material in an inviting form: using the springlike properties of the material, it is bent into shape and held in tension with the nuts. Its name refers to the fact that the chair assumes the temperature of the user.

85 Lamps Chandelier
Rody Graumans (Netherlands)
1993
85 lightbulbs, plastic-coated wire

Making much of relatively little, ordinary incandescent bulbs, clustered in bouquet-like form by a member of the Droog collective, become a stylish fixture without other adornment.

Babouin Fireplace, Claude Lalanne (France)
1984
Cast iron

Animal motifs were a constant in the work of Lalanne and her husband, François-Xavier, whose idiosyncratic designs—many of them in various handworked metals—were witty contrasts to the otherwise restrained furnishings in most Modernist interiors. None were made in large numbers: the fireplace was a limited edition of four. In the early years of the twenty-first century, 1980s Lalanne designs have enjoyed a revival.

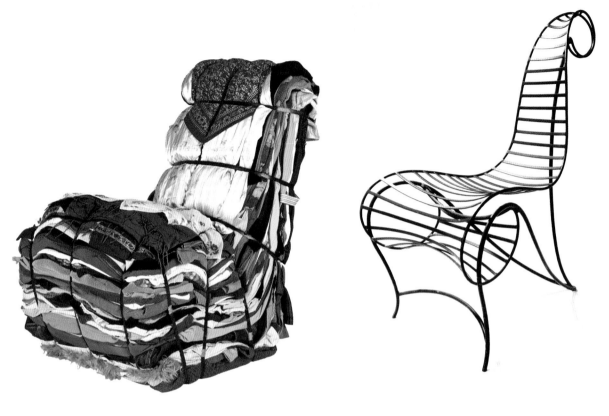

Rag Chair, Tejo Remy (Netherlands)
1991
Rags, metal strips

Assembled from the contents of fifteen bags of rags, no two of these chairs—by a member of the Droog collective—are exactly alike. The user, moreover, is given the option of adding discarded clothing to the design. Seen in the exhibition European Design Since 1985: Shaping the New Century. Remy, who has worked with the Droog design group since its formation in 1991, is known for repurposing commonplace materials into innovative designs.

Spine Chair, Andre Dubreuil (France)
1986
Bent and welded steel strips and rods

Dubreuil's most famous design, a deft marriage of tough industrial material and provocative organic form.

Tube Station Sofa, Julian Opie (United Kingdom)
1999
Tubular foam, fabric

Made in a limited edition of ten pieces, this
is perhaps a descendant of Joe Colombo's
1964 tube chair, in more restrained form.

REASSESSING MODERNISM

Toward the Millennium

A more permissive attitude toward diversity in design became apparent as the Postmodernism rebellion wound down, producing architecture, interiors, and furnishings that ran the gamut from stark to sensual. Designers rebelled against the kitsch of Memphis-inspired objects, and even their wittiest applications

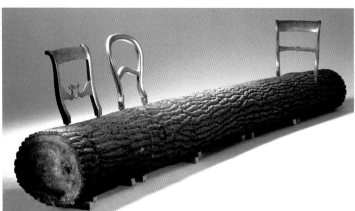

showed a new restraint. As the end of the century drew near, a look back at Modernism's "golden years" led to the rediscovery of decades-old designs, which for a while took precedence over actual innovations; instead of being reconceived, designs were recontextualized. Overall, the final design direction of the twentieth century is best characterized as Pluralism, in which historicist, contextualist, minimalist, and vernacular design jockeyed for position. The eclectic medley of styles produced no single archetype.

A key era in the reevaluation of the century was highlighted by Design 1935–1965: What Modern Was, the 1991

La Spiral, Louis Durot (France)
1992
Enamel-coated plastic

Tree-Trunk Bench, Jurgen Bey (Netherlands)
1999
Cast bronze, fallen tree trunk

The designer conceives the classical chair-back forms; the user supplies the tree into which they are installed; and the resulting object is a unique expression, though in a sense one example of a limited-edition

piece. The user participates in making the object but cannot alter the original intention of the designer, whose purpose was to engage the user in both thought and action. Bey's work was featured in European Design Since 1985: Shaping the New Century.

exhibition at Montreal's Musée des Arts Decoratifs. It called attention to the streamlined, biomorphic, historicist, ornamental, and expressionist aspects of twentieth-century modern design, as seen in works of the by-then celebrated designers who had defined it.

In architecture and building, applications of digital technology were being explored by innovators like Greg Lynn, Herzog and de Meuron, Sanaa, and others, revealing possibilities for structural forms that had previously existed only in the imagination. But it was with the opening of Frank Gehry's Guggenheim Museum in Bilbao, Spain, in 1997 that

such possibilities gained international attention. In what was later called the "Bilbao effect," a single piece of avant-garde architecture enabled the transformation of a city. The potential of architecture for such unprecedented influence would, in the next decade, transform several of its practitioners into so-called starchitect public figures—and would result in arresting public buildings that captivated (or dismayed) critics and made consumers more accepting of radical design—even, perhaps, in their own homes.

AK Table, Martin Szekely (France)
1999
Bété wood

Made in an edition of eight, plus two prototypes and two artist's proofs. The pedestals suggest movement, while the tabletop is clearly solid—a provocative treatment of a familiar form.

Cow Chair, Niels van Eijk
(Netherlands)
1997
Wood, cowhide

Natural cowhide draped like a coverlet over a simple chair frame. For Droog, this design treats familiar material in an unfamiliar fashion, challenging expectations without crossing the barrier between functioning and nonfunctioning design. Van Eijk and partner Miriam Van der Lubbe create furniture that forces the viewer to question its nature.

Getsuen Chair, Masanori Umeda (Japan)
1990
Upholstery, enameled steel, plastic,
chrome-plated brass

The floral form references Japanese tradition in an East-meets-West design from
an original member of the Memphis collaborative. This is one of three flower-form
seats that Umeda designed for quantity
production. Umeda worked in Italy for
the Castiglioni brothers and designed the
much-published "Tarawaya" seating furniture in the form of a boxing ring—usually
shown occupied by the Memphis members.

Amnesia Shelves, Andrea Branzi
(Italy)
1991
Enameled metal, tree trunk

Like much of Branzi's designs, these
incorporate natural branches into
Modernist forms. Made in an edition
of twenty.

Minimalism

The most austere direction in late-twentieth-century design was Minimalism, as dramatic a rejection of decoration per se as Postmodernism had been an embrace of all it represented. Minimalism was not so much a full-fledged movement as an adjunct one that developed in the wake of the art movement of the same name. Its trailblazers were architects John Pawson and Tadao Ando and designers Ward Bennett and Joseph D'Urso, who pared architecture and design to their abso-

lute essentials in constructing buildings and outfitting interiors. Architectural forms were starkly rectilinear, with broad expanses of glass for maximum light, and great swaths of concrete and hard materials like granite and slate. Interior space was carved out and sculpted into dramatic and occasionally disorienting landscapes. Walls were minimized or eliminated, exposing structural columns that became design elements in themselves. Areas of activity were defined by differences in floor levels, changes in wall texture, variations in carpet and surfacing materials, or layouts of furniture. Rooms were furnished with severe simplicity in a color palette that emphasized black,

Steel Furniture Table, Scott Burton (United States)
1978
Rusted hot-rolled steel

With a limited palette of unadorned material—in this case metal, but also stone or wood—sculptor Burton, since his first New York exhibition in 1975, has created minimalist abstract works of "sculpture-furniture": traditional forms that can function when not on display. This piece was produced in a limited edition of six, plus one artist's proof.

Glass Chair, Shiro Kuramata (Japan)
1976
Laminated glass

A new type of adhesive was used to secure the elements of a chair made entirely of glass slabs. Kuramata trained as an architect and later designed furniture for the Memphis collaborative.

Concrete Chair, Jonas Bohlin (Sweden)
1980
Concrete, steel

A limited-edition design using unaccustomed material in a familiar form. Also
made in wood. Bohlin is one of the younger
generation of Swedish designers exploring
new directions. His work crosses the line
between design and art.

Lamp (Oba-Q), Shiro Kuramata (Japan)
1972
Cut milk-white plastic sheet

I-Beam Occasional Table
Ward Bennett (United States)
c. 1978
Enameled steel

An ordinary construction beam transformed into assertively modern but
elegantly spare tables were among the
trademark furniture designs by Bennett,
a polymath artist/sculptor/display
designer/jewelry maker/interior designer
who pioneered Minimalist interiors,
most famously in the design of his
own bi-level apartment in New York's
landmark Dakota building.

Low Rolling Table, Joe D'Urso
(United States)
1980
Stainless steel, safety glass

D'Urso is one of the designers most
closely associated with the introduction of Minimalism in interior design.
A graduate of Pratt Institute, he was
a student and later associate of Ward
Bennett.

white, and gray, with depth and contrast provided by interplays of light and shadow. Wall surfaces were painted matte or high-gloss white, or were of textured stone or concrete. The vocabulary of furnishing materials was as likely to include granite, matte-finish metal, and natural stone as polished lacquer, commercial carpet, and etched glass. There were no extraneous elements, no ornament, and often no mark of human presence. In its ascetic, reductivist approach, Minimalism reflected the

influence of classical Japanese design—almost starkly simple, uncluttered, and sparsely furnished.

Minimalism did not represent an abandonment of Modernism but rather a highly intellectual distillation of its elements. Echoing the simplicity of Midcentury Modern and International Style design, it was far more rigorous. It was, however, difficult to sustain, and it gradually morphed into less austere translations that introduced subtle color and textural contrast; applications such as designer Christian Liaigre's use of gray walls, dark wood, and leather upholstery in hotel interiors were adapted for residential use. This empha-

Bed, Donald Judd (United States)
1993
Pine

Art becomes design in a spare form that relates directly to the artist's sculptures. Judd, who studied philosophy and worked as an art critic before becoming an artist, moved from painting to more material forms—geometric objects of wood, metal, concrete, and colored Plexiglas that were three-dimensional explorations in space. He is considered one of the important figures in Minimalist art, and the Whitney Museum

(1968 and 1988) and the Tate Modern (2004) have held solo exhibitions of his work.

Bend, Mårten Claesson (Sweden)
1999
Laminated birch or walnut veneer

The chair, reduced to its slimmest essentials, becomes almost a two-dimensional form.

sis on simplicity led naturally into another new development: the burgeoning movement toward sustainable and ecologically conscious design. Stimulated by a belated awareness of the problems caused by pollution and climate change—an issue that had been raised by environmentalists for several decades—the wider use of natural and environmentally sensitive materials and the avoidance of waste would become increasingly influential in design, affecting the planning, the materials, the fabrication, and the resulting appearance of interiors and furnishings.

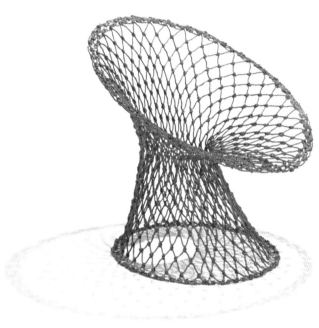

Parzival: A Chair with a Shadow
Robert Wilson (United States)
1987
Bleached birch, painted wood

Made in an edition of fifteen, this is one of a number of chairs designed over the past several decades by an artist best known for his work as a director of theater and opera, including *Einstein on the Beach*, with composer Philip Glass. Each of Wilson's chairs was designed as an accompaniment to one of his theatrical productions, but they are artworks rather than functional seating pieces.

Knotted Chair, Marcel Wanders(Netherlands)
1995
Carbon, aramide fiber cord, epoxy resin

Combining handcraft and technology, this award-winning design updates traditional macramé and is one version of a classic early work from Droog Design. Another version was shown in the exhibition European Design Since 1985: Shaping the New Century. Wanders, probably the best known of the current generation of Dutch designers, has designed interiors and household products and is the art director and co-owner of the avant-garde Dutch manufacturer Moooi.

MINIMALISM

The Minimalist interior was a stripped-down space with surfaces that might be high-gloss white, concrete, stone, or slate, and furnishings of a stringent simplicity. The look, as shown here, was rigorous and highly disciplined, with furniture as rectilinear as a Donald Judd sculpture, or geometric as the black-lacquer chairs. The almost-floating staircase has ultra-slim railings of matte steel. The color palette of black, white, and gray is relieved only rarely—here with lemon-yellow pillows—and accessories are kept to a minimum. Thus the space avoids both clutter and the idiosyncrasy of a personal touch.

Retro Design

One of the most noteworthy "new" directions in Modernism that emerged in the last decade of the twentieth century was the revival of midcentury styles and their incorporation into sophisticated, avant-garde architecture. Seen from the perspectives of time and distance, postwar furnishings became classics; and in politically and economically uncertain times, they were reassuring reminders of a more prosperous and optimistic past. The trend was perhaps jump-started, but certainly encouraged, by museum exhibitions such as Design Since 1945 and Design 1935–1965: What Modern Was. American Modernism was the focus of two important shows: Design in America: The Cranbrook Vision, 1925–1950 at the Detroit Institute of Arts in 1983 (later traveling to Paris and London as well as New York) and the 1983 High Styles: Twentieth-Century American Design at New York's Whitney Museum of American Art—the latter promoted as the first major exhibition to focus exclusively on American design. Even more significant, perhaps, was the modern design gallery that the Metropolitan Museum of Art opened in 1987. Rotating exhibits of highlights from the museum's collections—which included midcentury Scandinavian and Italian design as well as designs from earlier modern periods—were an important verification of Modernism's acceptance by the establishment.

Two other important exhibitions returned not only to earlier forms of Modernism but also specifically to studio crafts: New American Furniture: The Second Generation of Studio Furniture Makers, at the Museum of Fine Arts Boston in 1989, and Craft in the Machine Age, 1920–1945, in 1995 at New York's Museum of Contemporary Crafts (now the Museum of Arts and Design). The exhibitions raised the visibility of the craftsmen they featured, but more important, the museum venues helped to elevate the stature of craft itself.

The Miesian classicism of International Style open-plan residences returned in single-story, flat-roofed homes furnished

Hoop Chair, Hans Wegner (Denmark)
1986 (designed 1965)
Ash, flag halyard rope, upholstery
over foam

Perhaps considered too unconventional when it was first designed, this low-and-lazy design by a Scandinavian master moves conveniently on two caster-based rear legs.

Hanging Lamp, Model SP 1
Verner Panton (Denmark)
1969
Plastic, metal

One of the designer's distinctive pop-style pendant fixtures, with multiple ribbons, bubbles, or disk forms suspended on thin threads or wires. Panton, who worked in Arne Jacobsen's office for two years, designed some of the most avant-garde furniture to emerge from midcentury Denmark. In working with plastic and metal, he broke ranks with his conservative, wood-loving contemporaries.

Veranda Lounge Chair
Vico Magistretti (Italy)
1983
Striped fabric, enameled-steel base

Double J.M.F. Console Table,
Karl Springer (Germany)
ca. 1980
Laminated wood

Springer was best known for his use of exotic skins on tables, lamps, and occasional furniture. His designs combined modern silhouettes with luxury finishes recalling the Art Deco era.

Lounge Chair, Fabio Lenci (Italy)
1970
Glass, plastic, aluminum, leather

A comfort-minded version of see-through furniture from Italy, in an era when transparency was newly fashionable. The Italians and French had both introduced plastic blow-up chairs, which were a novelty varient on the idea.

Ball Chair, Eero Aarnio (Finland)
1963
Fiberglass, enameled aluminum, upholstery

Avant-garde in its time—and the antithesis of naturalistic, handcrafted Scandinavian design—this arresting form has a space-age look and has become a midcentury icon, featured in Design 1935–1965: What Modern Was and many museum collections. Aarnio's designs reflected pop culture more than his Nordic roots.

in retro-modern style, and looking much less extreme than when they were first introduced. A more anachronistic aspect of the revival was the frequent pairing of the brand-new and the newly revived: avant-garde architecture and midcentury furnishings. Now-classic pieces by Arne Jacobsen and Verner Panton, Charles and Ray Eames, and George Nakashima were newly ubiquitous in interiors whose architectural surrounds resembled abstract sculpture. The combination worked surprisingly well, but the repeated use of the same vocabulary of objects underscored the scarceness of original new furniture.

In helping to stifle innovation, this nostalgia for midcentury style had its downside: many of the new products it generated seemed mere reprises of familiar tunes. All of the important exhibitions traveled to several museum venues, accompanied by lavishly illustrated catalogues, which were equally influential in raising awareness of, and interest in, the periods and the designs on which they were focused.

Mayan Sofa, Harvey Probber (United States)
1983
Upholstery over wood
A trademark piece by a midcentury
designer who often drew on traditional
sources. Though modern in form,
Probber's designs were more svelte
than severe.

Harbingers of Change

Though the revival of midcentury design threatened to become as repetitive as its original applications, plumbing the past also led to the rediscovery of other earlier styles. In search of the new, designers sometimes embraced the old-but-forgotten or the never-appreciated, and there were also welcome signs of genuinely forward-thinking ideas. Furniture with intricately crafted details, made from unconventional materials or using unaccustomed techniques, presaged the evolution of a new genre

 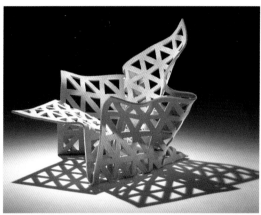

of experimental and conceptual furniture that would grow exponentially in the new century. Along with this, designers in countries with strong national heritages—including France, Italy, Spain, and the Scandinavian nations—were nurturing a new generation's approach to their traditional design cultures.

Spurred by new technology and changes in family composition and lifestyles, domestic environments were changing as well. Signs of the times—and the times to come—were seen in residences like Rem Koolhaas's Maison à Bordeaux, Shigeru Ban's Curtain Wall House, and others shown in the Museum of Modern Art's 1999 exhibition The Un-Private House. These

Waves, Anne-Mette Jensen and Marten Ernst (Denmark)
1994
Wood, filling, leather or cowhide

Bless You Chair, Louise Campbell (Denmark)
1999
Felt, gelatin sheets

A technically sophisticated design, melding a single square sheet of felt with 750 ultra-thin sheets of gelatin into a flexible form inspired by a crumpled handkerchief, then laser-cut into a decorative openwork pattern. In 2006, Campbell was given an "Interiors Maverick Award" by *Wallpaper* magazine.

and other designs by firms including Diller + Scofidio, Herzog & de Meuron, and Hariri & Hariri showed the ways in which architecture was encompassing the changing aspects of family and domestic life.

Lest an influential era be forgotten, in 2001 the Brooklyn Museum launched the exhibition Vital Forms: American Art and Design in the Atomic Age, 1940–1960, a reminder of one aspect of design that had fueled the creative output of the midcentury years.

Vermelha Chair, Fernando and Humberto Campana (Brazil)
1998
Handwoven dyed cotton rope, epoxy powder-coated steel, aluminum

Woven threads are formed into ropes, which are in turn woven into upholstery in a piece that looks randomly assembled but is in fact a highly structured design. The work of the Campana brothers focuses on transforming familiar materials and sometimes found objects—using traditional artisanal techniques—into pieces that are distinctively original and filled with personality. The Design Museum, London, staged a retrospective of their work in 2004,

and they were named Designer of the Year by Design Miami, 2008.

Oto Chair, Peter Karpf (Norway)
1960
Natural, stained, or lacquered beech

A sinuous shape of one-piece construction, this chair is formed without screws or joints.

Palio Table Lamp, Perry King (United Kingdom) and Santiago Miranda (Spain)
ca. 1990s

Two central milk-glass shades in a polished and enameled metal housing

Armchair, Pawel Grunert (Poland)
1994
Wicker, rope, resin

Conceptual take on the conventional club chair: strands of wicker, wrapped in a tight cluster like a sheaf of wheat, with seating area sculpted out in the center. Grunert's ecologically sensitive furniture and sculpture makes imaginative use of sustainable materials and recycled objects.

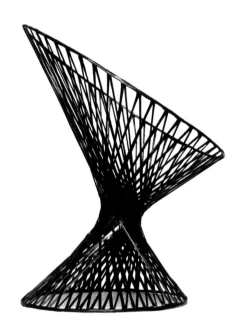

Sushi Sofa, Fernando and Humberto
Campana (Brazil)
2003
Felt, textiles, plastic, EVA, steel

A variation of the wrapped-roll
concept, here with stiffer materials
to create a more rigid seating surface.
Made in a limited edition of seven,
with two artist's proofs and three
prototypes.

Spun Chair, Mathias Bengtsson
(Denmark)
2002
Carbon fiber

Space-age material, intricately woven
to suggest the look of handcraft, but
achieved with technologically advanced
computerized methods adapted from
aeronautical production. One of
Bengtsson's works in this material and
technique was included in European
Design Since 1985: Shaping the New
Century

REINVENTING MODERNISM: THE TWENTY-FIRST CENTURY

When books of design history are rewritten, the Modernism of the twenty-first century will be defined as markedly different from that of its predecessors. It already is. The design historian Paul Greenhalgh once said of the twentieth century, "Modernism meant anything you wanted it to." Though this was arguable in its original context, that statement applies unquestionably to design thus far in the twenty-first century. The definition of Modernism—in fact, the definition of design itself—is more evanescent and more flexible than it has ever been, embracing a world of cultural pluralism and an unprecedented spirit of openness and curiosity.

My Beautiful Backside Sofa
Nipa Doshi (India) and Jonathan
Levien (United Kingdom)
2008
Hardwood, vari-density polyurethane
foam and fiberfill, upholstery, enameled
buttons, walnut

Double Bottle, Barber Osgerby
(United Kingdom)
2007
White Calacatta or black Marquinia
marble
This design by two Royal College of
Art graduates, partners since 1996, was
named best table of 2007 by *Wallpaper*
magazine. Also made in a single-bottle
version: the top and bases are connected
with a conic joint.

As the pugnacity of Postmodernism faded, a more relaxed attitude toward formulas, doctrines, and manifestos evolved, and the boundaries of design now seem limitless. In this digitized age of test-tube materials and futuristic technologies, almost anything is possible—and, perhaps more important, virtually anything has become acceptable.

The aggressive marketing of design products and design practitioners has opened a dialogue that includes the general public. For the first time since nineteenth-century design reform, design is once more a plangent subject of public interest, generating heated debate, criticism, and continuous media coverage. This is all to the good, as a design-conscious public encourages designers to stretch their creative muscles to reach into uncharted territory. In this climate, they have conceived objects ranging from exceptional to bizarre—but at either extreme, impossible to dismiss.

Lacking the perspective of distance, it is too soon to make definitive statements about particular movements, enduring trends, or archetypal forms that will become the landmarks of this century. But it is already possible to identify several clear directions and many designs worth at least a second look. Some of the new directions may portend historic changes; others may have only marginal influence. But all feed into the germinating mix that promises this will be a century to reckon with.

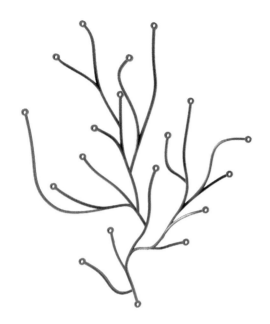

Algue, Ronan & Erwan Bouroullec (France)
2004
Injection-molded plastic
Inspired by nature, the basic design is a small motif, multiples of which snap together to form a large-scale weblike object with many possibilities for different sizes and configurations. Shown in the exhibition European Design Since 1985: Shaping the New Century.

At Paris's Salon de Meuble in 1998, the Bouroullec brothers were awarded the Grand Prix du Design, and in 2002 they were named Designers of the Year. Their work is in the collections of major museums in America and Europe.

Tam Tam, Matteo Thun (Italy)
2002
Rotational-molded polyethylene

CONTEXT: THE FIRST DECADE

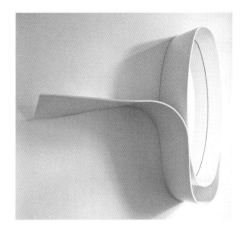

The new century opened in a state of disequilibrium, with the collapse of the dot-com industry, the aftermath of the Soviet Union's demise, and China's explosive emergence as a world power. Wars in Iraq and Afghanistan, genocide in Africa, and the tragedy of September 11 made the first decade one of political disruption and economic uncertainty. As it drew to a close, international conflict and widespread recession suggested that a return to earlier, more optimistic times would not be easy, or even possible. The stresses of real life led to escapist fantasy and revival styles—in fashion, theater, film, and music—as technology continued to transform virtually every aspect of public and private life. Technology interceded in human interaction as email, texting, Facebook, and Twitter supplanted face-to-face, even voice-to-voice, communication. For its youngest generations, society was becoming increasingly depersonalized, or at least transposed into a new dimension in cyberspace. A cornucopia of unrelated design styles reflected this fragmented world and the need to find some means of expressing individuality and emotion.

Despite the drawbacks of the digital age, continuing advances in computer engineering have opened possibilities that stagger the imagination, leading designers to become explorers in search of new forms, new materials, and new techniques with which to translate need into object. Their achievements are reflected not only in the implements of everyday life—"smart" phones, electronic readers, hybrid cars, and more—but also in visionary architecture, interiors, furniture, and lighting. Sophisticated software and space-age materials enable architects and designers to execute almost anything that a fertile imagination can conceive: ingenious forms and structures never before possible, in materials only recently invented, to use in reconfiguring the past or inventing the future.

DESIGN AFTER MODERNISM

Why/Why Not, Philip Michael Wolfson (United States)
2009
LG Hi-Mac acrylic, mirror
From an edition of eight.

Flora, Tord Boontje (Netherlands)
2009
Sheet metal, stainless steel or copper

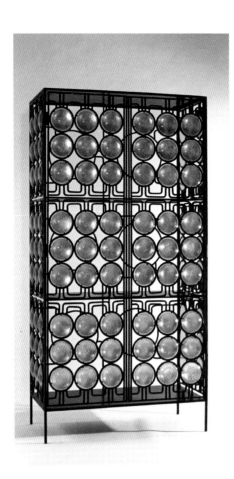

Honey Silver Etagere
Christophe Côme (France)
2003
Metal, glass rondels, silver leaf
Handcraft mixes rough and smooth, dark and light, matte and reflective surfaces. This artist is a specialist in metal and glass works.

NON Chairs and Table, Komplot (Denmark)
2000
Monoblock molded in PUR-rubber
A material associated with flexibility is unexpectedly rigid in this translation of a simple wood chair form, shown (without the table) in the exhibition European Design Since 1985: Shaping the New Century. Dane Poul Christiansen and Russian-born Boris Berlin, who formed Komplot in Copenhagen in 1987, began this century by exploring new approaches to chair design through innovative uses of materials and technology.

Grenouille Table, Hella Jongerius (Netherlands)
2009
Walnut and transparent blue enamel
The anthropomorphic form of the frog leg is both a double entendre and a whimsical accent for an otherwise simple table.

In this, technology has provided not just the most extraordinary potential but also the most critical challenges for design today and in the years to come.

Sustainable design, popularly known as Green Design, gained ground in the 1990s and has exploded in the new century. More than a movement, it is an approach to all aspects of design and, indeed, of lifestyle, seeking to minimize the impact of humans on our environment. Its principles, the roots of which date back to Rachel Carson and Victor Papanek, were first promulgated by William McDonough with the Hannover Principles, called a "Bill of Rights for the Planet," for EXPO 2000 in Germany, and expanded by McDonough and Michael

Braungart in *Cradle to Cradle: Remaking the Way We Make Things* (2002). As the single most important international design direction of the twenty-first century—and the only one with potentially vast consequences for the life of the planet— Green Design has changed the way architects and designers conceive and implement their ideas. In the process, it has generated considerable innovation as well as social benefits. It has led to certification programs, eco-labeling systems in products, and the prestigious LEED program, initiated in 2000 to certify environmentally responsible buildings and design professionals.

BDI Relax, Björn Dahlström (Sweden)
2000
Fabric, down, and tubular steel
The design combines a chaise with a sleeping bag, including padding and a zipper front.

Flower, Pierre Paulin (France)
2009
Polycarbonate, fabric or leather cushions
The latest design by an early Modernist, in a characteristically organic form but a more advanced material than the bent-wire and stretched-fabric seating that he pioneered.

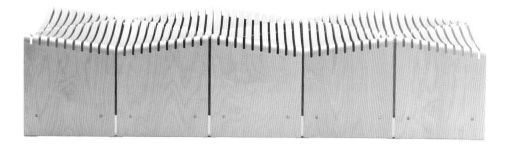

Twister, Yuriko Takahashi
(Denmark, b. Japan)
2002
Laminated birch or black-stained
veneer, chromed-steel linking brackets

The wavy surface gives a feeling of
movement to a seating design that can
be used in many different configurations. Seen in the headquarters of the
New York Times, Takahashi's designs
emphasize curves and motion.

Tavolino, Alessandro Mendini (Italy)
2008
Fiberglass, glass mosaic tiles

A recent work by one of Italy's pioneer
avant-garde designers. Made in a
limited edition of eight plus two artist's
proofs and two prototypes.

360° Family Desk Unit, Konstantin Grcic
(Germany)
2010
Aluminum, steel, painted MDF

Function reasserts primacy over form in an
ensemble of designs that swivel to encourage
movement rather than static positions—
a seat that is something between a stool
and a chair, and a companion table.

Avec, Brigitte Loof (Denmark)
2007
Fabric over polyester foam, blockboard,
tubular steel

Hinged sides adjust to four positions to
convert a sofa into either chaise or daybed.

Double-Chair, Chris Rucker (United States)
2005
Oriented strand board

The elegant tete-a-tete transformed with
commonplace material and minimalist
form. Made in an edition of eight plus
one prototype.

Extruded Chair, Tom Dixon
(United Kingdom, b. Tunisia)
2007
Extruded PETG plastic

Fragile in its openwork design, yet providing
sturdy and flexible seating, this was made in
a limited edition of twelve.

Masters Chair, Philippe Starck
(France)
2010
Batch-dyed polypropylene

Paying homage to the work of three
design masters, this chair combines the
forms of their most iconic designs: Arne
Jacobsen's #7, Charles Eames's Eiffel,
and Eero Saarinen's Tulip.

20/30, Raphaël Charles (Belgium)
2008
Foam, PE, and felt

A cross between a rug and a sculptural
piece, this questions the relevance of
function to design. Made in a limited
edition of twenty plus three prototypes.

Meander Coffee Table
Mattia Bonetti (France, b. Switzerland)
2009
Patinated bronze, clear acrylic top

Made in a limited edition of twenty.
Bonetti, who became known in the
1980s for his distinctively atavistic
designs in collaboration with Elizabeth
Garouste, uses rigid materials to create
elegant objects of art furniture.

THE DESIGNERS

The design community itself has also changed. More people are engaging in design—not only those trained in the discipline but also those from related fields who are contributing or collaborating to create architecture, design interiors, and conceive objects. Some have become international celebrities, contributing to the prestige of the professions in which they work, but most labor in less lofty circumstances, working alone, in pairs, or in small collectives. They experiment with tools and technology from other industries, finding applications unforeseen by the original inventors and remaking their surroundings to suit their specifications.

This new freedom has enabled designers to work across disciplines; the specialist has been replaced by the crossover creator, who may with equal facility express him/herself in media from architecture to interiors to furniture to decorative objects and displays. These practitioners are as much engineers or technicians as they are artists, artisans, and designers. Led by Ron Arad, Marc Newson, and a handful of other high-profile innovators, they design objects that may simultaneously encompass luxury and functionality, excess and restraint. At the same time, many among them are addressing sociocultural issues with a newly awakened, or reawakened, sense of social responsibility: they believe that design can help to change the world, and they aspire to contribute to that change.

DESIGN AFTER MODERNISM

Single Poltrona with Cover, Jamie Hayon (Spain)
2008
Armchair back in medium-density polyethylene, upholstery in Capitone leather, lacquer

From a collection of designs, called Showtime, inspired by MGM musicals, this inviting seating piece marries organic form and classical details with modern materials. An optional cover outfits the piece for outdoor use. Hayon is one of the young designers whose work crosses the lines between decoration and art, with projects that have included toys and ceramics as well as interiors and furniture.

Black Hole Table, Marc Newson
(Australia)
ca. 2006
Carbon fiber

Conceived in 1988, the one-piece
table was finally produced in 2006 in
a limited edition of ten. The legs seem
to flow out of recesses in the rounded-
triangle top.

Two-Piece Sectional Sofa
Vladimir Kagan (United States)
2005
Wood frame, boucle and finely
ribbed fabric, velvet pillows

THE ARCHITECTURE

Most of today's modern buildings can be seen as descendants of Frank Lloyd Wright's tradition: they are continuums of inter-related spaces rather than a series of independent entities, and Wright's principle of integration into the landscape—the idea of context—is almost always a given. The key tenets of Modernist architecture endure, but they are implemented in a manner inconceivable without technology. Using materials and methods not available to their midcentury predecessors, architects in the twenty-first century work in partnership with engineers and scientists to create and construct buildings with ribbon bands of metal, serpentine glass facades, movable panels, and gravity-

DESIGN AFTER MODERNISM

defying forms made possible by techniques of computer modeling. In the decade and more since Gehry's Guggenheim Bilbao, architects have used the computer to create an extraordinary range of forms. There are buildings shaped as coils, stacked boxes, jagged pyramids, amoeba-like curves, or interlocking volumes, with overhangs, skylights, folded rooflines, multilevel ceilings, and angular walls. These energetic shapes seem to be moving while standing in place. Not just Gehry and Koolhaas but also Norman Foster, Richard Rogers, Herzog & de Meuron, Sanaa, Santiago Calatrava, Zaha Hadid, Peter Zumthor, Steven

Org, Fabio Novembre (Italy)
2001
Steel, flexible polypropylene rope, clear glass, satin-finish stainless steel

With some fixed legs of rope-covered steel and others of flexible rope, the table seems almost to float on spider like limbs—a provocative piece in different heights and sizes by an architect who has designed stores, showrooms, and restaurants as well as furniture.

Spirit House Chair, Daniel Libeskind
(United States, b. Poland)
2007
Brushed and polished stainless steel, leather

A rare venture into furniture design by the architect known for his use of stainless steel in organic buildings. Made in an edition of 100.

Holl, Thomas Mayne, and others have produced electrifying structures—many of them museums—that take architecture to a new level. Buildings need no longer be passive enclosures; they can harness solar energy, recycle waste and water, and con-

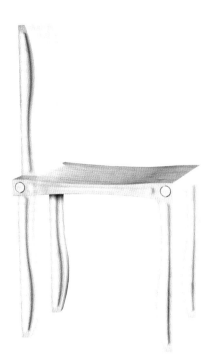

trol illumination. In addition to such practical considerations, "smart houses" can boast more esoteric features: walls that extend or retract, change color or opacity on command, adapt to variations in climate, project images or pattern, even emit scent—responding to the occupant's needs by means of a central computerized control. And they can do all this while being ecologically considerate. Though not always related to the design of interiors, such architecture cannot help but influence them, demanding equally assertive treatments—or self-effacingly noncompetitive ones.

10-Unit System, Shigeru Ban (Japan)
2009
UPM ProFi wood-plastic composite
A single L-shape component, the basis of a unique modular system, is used to assemble this chair as well as other furniture forms. It is made from a new composite material of recycled paper and plastic, environmentally sustainable and recyclable. Ban, an internationally known architect, is best known for his "Curtain Wall" house (1995) and his highly original use of cardboard tubes for architectural structures.

Origami Chair, Philip Michael Wolfson (United States)
2007
Gold-leafed acid-patinated sheet steel
Skillfully folded and golden-surfaced, steel here becomes the most elegant of materials—made in an edition of eight. An American architect now based in London, he worked with Zaha Hadid on a number of projects before establishing his own practice in 1991. Influenced by the Italian Modernists, Wolfson manipulates hard-edged materials like metal into fluid sculptural forms or translates computer-drawn silhouettes in carbon fiber for furniture that is also sculpture.

Neo Chester Sofa, Patrick Naggar
(France)
2008
Wood, foam, upholstery

An architect and designer, Naggar has
worked in Europe and the United States,
and is represented in prominent museum
collections.

Calder's Table, Ali Tayar
(United States, b. Turkey)
2003
Cast bronze, painted MDF

The disorienting angle of the legs suggests
movement—hence the name recalling an
Alexander Calder sculpture. Works by
Tayar, an architect, have been featured at
the Museum of Modern Art exhibitions
Mutant Materials and Workspheres, and in
European Design Since 1985: Shaping the
New Century. In 2009 Tayar was the recipi-
ent of a National Design Award from the
Cooper-Hewitt National Design Museum.

Aqua Table, Zaha Hadid
(United Kingdom, b. Iraq)
2005
Satin-matte and high-gloss painted
glass reinforced polyester

The undulating form of this monolithic
work suggests a flowing liquid, allowing the
horizontal tabletop to melt into three vertical
supports. Irregularities in the silicone-gel
tabletop create subtle gradations in color
that seem to give movement to the piece.
Produced in a limited edition, this form is
clearly related to the sweeping silhouettes
of Hadid's recent architecture.

Pebbles, Claesson Koivisto Rune
(Sweden)
2001
Metal, poplar, polyurethane foam,
bi-elastic fixed fabric

Mårten Claesson, Eero Koivisto,
and Ola Rune, fellow students at
Stockholm's Konstfack, are probably
Sweden's leading architecture and
design firm. In 2004 they were the first
Swedish firm to exhibit at the Venice
Architecture Biennale.

Jean, Antonio Citterio (Italy)
2009
Tubular steel, steel sections, flexible
cold-shaped polyurethane foam,
polyester fiber, painted die-cast
extruded aluminum

THE INTERIORS

More than ever before, the interiors of the twenty-first century are expressions of individual style—whether that of the designers or the clients. And there have never before been so many styles from which to choose. An increasing proportion of them

fall within the general rubric of modernity—a term that remains the best available label for this new generation of design. But this is not your grandmother's Modernism. It is redefined and reenergized, accepts variations, embraces combinations, and encourages diversity.

Whether a glass-walled aerie, a dressed-up loft, a modified minimal retreat, a classical cocoon, a sensual surround, or an avant-garde space with structural interfaces, today's interiors are likely to be harmonious blends of many notes. Partial walls, floating staircases, and exposed columns are familiar accents, as are materials such as concrete, granite, slate, and

Long Island Chaise, Lin Jing (China)
2005
Stainless steel
Made in an edition of eight.

Lamp, Claesson Koivisto Rune (Sweden)
2010
DuraPulp (paper and bioplastic composite), cast iron
Traditional and modern materials assembled into a bold contemporary lighting design.

Polder Sofa, Hella Jongerius (Netherlands)
2005
Wood, belt upholstery, polyurethane foam, microfiber and polyester wool, sand, buttons

Flexible armrest cushions, weighted with sand, can be rearranged into random forms—a touch of inconsistency that suggests the hand of the maker in a machine-made object. Seen in a major 2010 retrospective of the designer's work in Rotterdam, Netherlands. Jongerius is known for melding elements of design and craft in work that weaves traditional elements into contemporary forms.

Claustra, François Bauchet (France)
2008
Oregon pine

A limited edition of eight plus two artist's proofs and two prototypes.

Nanook Chair, Philippe Bestenheider (Switzerland)
2009
Printed synthetic material, lacquered steel

A lively graphic is digitally printed onto the machine-molded surface, hexagon-shaped to suggest a snowflake, for a lively looking chair with an added message: the graphic covering, a skin of sorts, recalls the tanning of a quadriped's hide. The name of the chair is taken from a classic documentary film in which Inuits cover themselves with animal skin.

matte-finish metal. The maximization of natural light is one of several considerations dictated by the growing commitment to Green Design and sustainability. Another is the use of durable, recyclable, or otherwise environmentally sensitive textiles, surfaces, and finishes. Styles of the past are still retained or revived, but they are most often used in provocative partnerships: polished steel with studio craft, new limited editions with Midcentury Modern, Bauhaus with eighteenth century, Art Deco with avant-garde. Whatever the style, these interiors embrace electronics: computers and audiovisual equipment take a prime position, even center stage, in twenty-first-century living spaces.

Any attempt to chart a single direction for today's interior design is made impossible by the grab bag of ethnic and

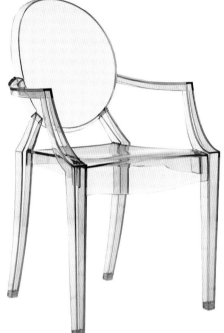

multicultural style influences that reflect the much-vaunted diversity of the global community. These influences have ushered in a return of ornament—although many designers, wary of ornament's uncomfortable history with Modernism, are hesitant in its application. Contemporary interiors frequently use texture in its place, or play with pattern mixes in adventurous and unexpected ways. Color directions are equally diverse, from understated to assertive—producing rooms that are, at one end of the spectrum, subtly monochromatic, and at the other, high-intensity extravagant.

Bridge Table, Joris Laarman
(Netherlands)
2010
Aluminum, tungsten carbide

Laarman's work is in the collections of more than twenty museums in Europe and America. His designs combine advanced technology with naturalistic forms.

Louis Ghost Armchair
Philippe Starck (France)
2002
Injection-molded polycarbonate, clear or opaque

A technically innovative translation of a classic period design, formed from a single mold. Shown in the exhibition European Design Since 1985: Shaping the New Century. One of the best-selling plastic chairs produced in recent years.

Dervish Lamp, Philippe Malouin
(United Kingdom, b. Canada)
2009
Fan structure in metal, PMMA,
300 felt strips

When the fan is turned on, the strips
spin to suggest dancers' skirts, in a
whimsical fillip for a functional design.

Karbon Chaise Lounge
Konstantin Grcic (Germany)
2008
Carbon fiber

A sleekly simple translation of
traditional form in an ultra-modern
material. Made in a limited edition
of twelve plus two prototypes.

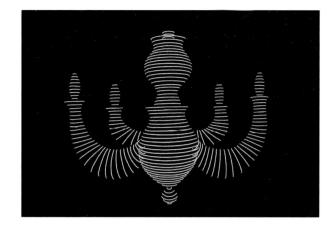

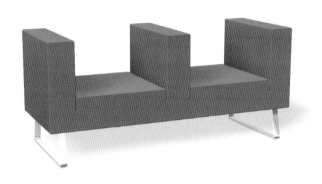

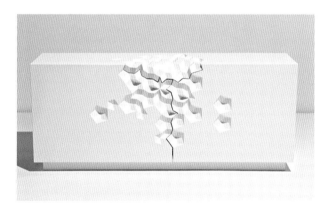

Viper, Lajsa Nordstrom and
Henning Eklund (Sweden)
2007
Compression-molded birch, oak,
or melamine, tubular steel

HB, Olivier Peyricot (France)
2008
Carrara marble, plastic-coated steel
Produced in an edition of eight plus
one artist's proof.

Ragno, Marcus Tremonto
(United States)
2006
Electroluminescent wire, Perspex
A classic chandelier form is outlined
in wire and sandwiched between
layers of Perspex, creating a
three-dimensional illusion with a
two-dimensional piece. More art
than design, Tremonto's works play
with the possibilities of illumination. All are limited editions—this
one, of ten.

E-Seat, Thomas Eriksson
(Denmark)
2002
Upholstery, cold-foam, wood, steel

Quasi Cabinet, Aranda/Lasch
(United States)
2007
Lacquered wood, metal

Sharpei, Morten Voss (Denmark)
2008
Upholstery, underframe in lacquered MDF

The carefully wrinkled upholstery recalls the distinctive surface of the Chinese breed after which it was named.

Loveseat Lounge, Riikka Paasonen and Petra Majantie (Finland)
2000
Fabric, foam, aluminum

FURNITURE: THE NEW FACE OF MODERNISM

Furniture design has broken the restraints of Modernism, to redefine and reenergize both the practice and the style. It has encouraged visionary concepts, manipulation of materials, and disruption of forms. In so doing, it has produced objects of diversity, not homogeneity, "of exploration, not emulation," of pleasure, not practicality. They go beyond the mere idea of form and function—though many of them function perfectly

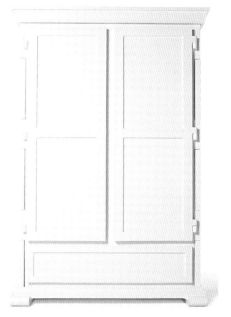

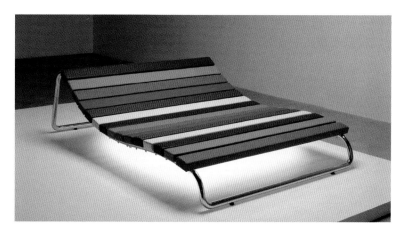

well—to offer the challenge of interpreting them, responding emotionally to them, even interacting with them. Such furniture is unquestionably of the moment, but it is altogether independent of fashion. While designers are looking to the past as well as to the future, many of their creations bear no resemblance to objects of any previous generation, and therefore past criteria for evaluating them have little meaning. The resulting confusion has generated ambivalence about nomenclature—as evidenced by the title of the 2004 Cooper-Hewitt Museum exhibition Design ≠ Art.

Nevertheless, museum exhibitions have encouraged

Chaise Lounge from the Collection for the New Economy, Johanna Grawunder (United States)
2006
Vinyl, chrome-plated tubular steel, fluorescent tube

Light enhances the ordinary materials and conventional form here. The chaise was introduced in a Milan exhibition called New Positions: Office Furniture for the New Economy and was made in an edition of twelve. Most of Grawunder's limited-edition works, like this one, explore the possibilities of integrating light and color for effects that transform furniture into art. Grawunder was a partner in Sottsass Associati before opening her own studios in San Francisco and Milan.

Paper Cupboard, Studio Job—Job Smeets and Nynke Tynagel (Belgium/Netherlands)
2005
Honeycomb panels, paper, cardboard, polyurethane lacquer

The concept: a traditional handcrafted form fabricated by machine with modern materials, and shipped flat-packed for practicality. From a collection including a buffet, low cabinet, wardrobe, and screen—an homage to classical style and a remembrance of childhood play with paper cutouts. Job Smeets and Nynke Tynagel formed Studio Job in 2002 after graduating from Design Academy Eindhoven and are among the most-admired designers of concept-based furniture.

Madam Rubens, Frank Willems (Netherlands)

2004

Wood, foam mattresses, polyurethane

In an ingenious recycling application, discarded (and cleaned) foam mattresses and broken chairs are assembled into a quirky seating piece, then coated with polyurethane for durability. A variation of the design was made as a limited edition.

Plus Unit, Werner Aisslinger (Germany)

2001

Injection-molded ABS, extruded and polished or painted aluminum

Award-winning industrial designer Aisslinger is known for his use of new materials and technology, which he has applied to furniture, architecture, and product design. His 1996 Juli chair, the first to use polyurethane integral foam, was the initial German design to be chosen as a permanent exhibit at the Museum of Modern Art in 1964.

Yesbox, Yrjö Wiherheimo (Finland)

2006

Upholstery, foam, tubular steel

A variation on the usual movable modular seating: individual seating units, with or without arms, become a fixed multi-seat unit when set into a steel base.

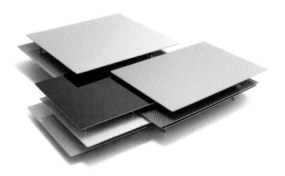

Lunario Table, Claesson Koivisto Rune
(Sweden)
2005
Wooden structure, foam, textile, metal

Skid Row, Philippe Malouin
(United Kingdom, b. Canada)
2009
Tubular steel, birch wood balls,
shock cord

Made in an edition of twelve plus one
prototype.

Stingray, Thomas Pedersen (Denmark)
2008
Plastic or laminate shell, steel frame

Grid Coffee Table and Lamp-Side Table
Chris Lehrecke (United States)
2008
Walnut

A modern design in the handcraft tradition
by a young designer-craftsman.

Etage Tables, Eero Koivisto (Sweden)
2009
Laminated MDF, high-gloss
Formica AR, chrome

A random-layered effect for a table whose
elements are precisely fixed.

interest in all segments of the design spectrum: for example, the Museum of Fine Arts Boston staged The Maker's Hand: American Studio Furniture, 1940–1990 in 2003, while the Denver Art Museum mounted a more avant-garde–focused U.S. Design, 1975–2000 in 2002, followed by a cosponsored European Design Since 1985: Shaping the New Century with the Indianapolis Art Museum in 2008.

Art, science, and technology have coalesced in furniture designed on the computer, and made with additive layer fabrication (rapid prototyping), which fabricates objects directly from computer drawings in forms impossible to achieve with ordinary machines. Other methodologies being used in furniture include motion-capture and three-dimensional printing; computer algorithms that generate random forms or patterns; automated laser-cutting; electrolytic baths; rotation molding and stereolithography; and techniques from unrelated industries, including processes adopted from chemistry, engineering, and biotechnology. Materials are incredibly varied—familiar

Orgy Sofa and Ottoman
Karim Rashid (United States, b. Egypt)
2009
Wood, cold foam, flameproof fiber,
fabric, chromed steel

Bench, Studio Job—Job Smeets and
Nynke Tynagel (Belgium/Netherlands)
2006
Macassar ebony, laser-cut bird's-eye
maple inlays

Straddling the line between design and
art, Studio Job created a suite of furniture ornamented with hand-cut marquetry of fossilized skeletons, and called
it the Perished collection: a celebration/
commemoration of extinct species.
The table, screen, pedestal, and this
bench are a limited edition of six.

Item, Patrick Jouin (France)
2010
Wood, foam, fabric

The unusual shape is achieved by avoid-
ing the use of right angles—a modular
system with fourteen pieces to allow for
many possible configurations.

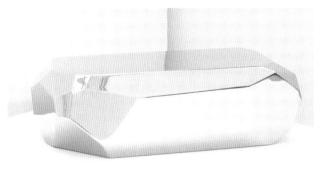

ones used in unfamiliar ways and others not traditionally seen in furniture—felt, kraft paper, recycled cork, leather scraps, old newspapers, even glass fragments—or more arcane media including polyamide and polypropylene, photopolymer liquid, carbon fiber, resin, thermoplastics, fiber optics, Tyvek, Kevlar, vacuum-blown metals, sculpted glass, and light-emitting diodes.

Many of the most intriguing new designs are part furniture and part experiment in structure or materials, using the design studio as a laboratory. The Cooper-Hewitt Museum explored experimental design in its 2006 Design Life Now exhibition; and a more comprehensive and thought-provoking 2008 Museum of Modern Art exhibition, Design and the Elastic Mind, showed objects—some still laboratory-bound but others actually being produced—that were enabled by science and technology to interact with the user, control the environment, or benefit society. This exhibition focused on designers' explorations into heretofore-uncharted territories to create entirely new types of objects—what curator Paola Antonelli described as "a portrait, a few years in advance, of where the world is going."

At the other end of the spectrum, that same year London's Victoria & Albert Museum showcased furniture as fantasy in Telling Tales, exhibiting objects by designers such as Maarten

Dear Ingo, Ron Gilad (Israel)
2003
Powder-coated steel

Titled in homage to celebrated lighting designer Ingo Maurer, a cluster of sixteen office-type task lamps make a chandelier with infinitely adjustable, spiderlike arms.

Rock Table, Arik Levy
(France, b. Israel)
2005
Mirror-polished stainless steel

A signature form by a designer whose career has encompassed graphic arts, sculpture, theater and ballet sets, exhibitions, as well as furniture and industrial design. Made in an edition of twelve. Levy's work has been exhibited at the Centre Pompidou, the Museum of Modern Art, and the Victoria & Albert Museum.

Baas, Studio Job, and Tord Boontje that were intended as personal statements or expressions of ideas. Though the exhibition concepts were polar opposites, the designs in both were objects to think about, to stimulate, to challenge—well beyond conventional definitions of what we expect furniture to look like and to do.

Designers of furniture are freer in their investigations into form; where strict linearity once defined the avant-garde, mathematically calculated curves are now equally acceptable. Some pieces are quirky and iconoclastic—furniture as self-expression. Some are conceived by manipulating existing pieces: disassembling, wrapping, piercing, painting, or decorating them. There are deconstructed forms that have been crushed, fractured, or distorted to become almost unrecognizable. Traditional archetypes have been abandoned or subverted, conventions flouted, boundaries dissolved. Uptown-elegant or downtown-tough, overstuffed or svelte, frivolous or sedate, this is furniture of many different inspirations and almost any mood—little wonder that collecting design has become akin to collecting fine art. As art, craft, and design have commingled, many works are impossible to label as either one or the other—hence the somewhat awkward terms "design/art," "art furniture," or even "concept furniture" to describe objects that fit neither category and in which aesthetic or intellectual considerations take priority over function.

In transcending the focus on function, such designs as these subvert the idea of what furniture was once intended to be. They challenge its vocabulary and demand an expanded view of what may be labeled Modern as well as, perhaps, a new definition of what we call design.

Despite this extraordinary range, and the confusion it engenders, several specific directions—which cannot precisely be designated as styles—have manifested themselves. They are all very much of the moment, and possibly of many moments to come.

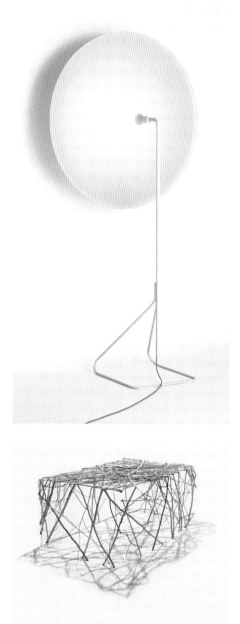

Parabola, Pierre Charpin (France)
2008
Metallic tube, matte-resin lampshade
Made in a limited edition of eight plus two artist's proofs and two prototypes.

Design by Pressure, Front Design (Sweden)
2000
Pressurized tree branches
Front Design, a Stockholm-based design group of four women, focuses on process rather than product. In this case, branches are placed under high pressure to create a new material, assembled into a table that casts a graceful shadow and appears as fragile as the original elements from which it was made. Other projects by Front Design have explored designing with sunlight, motion, gravity, and temperature.

Toot, Piero Lissoni (Italy)
2009
Polyurethane foam, down, die-cast
polished aluminum, fabric or leather

A multifunction system that can be
assembled with or without sides, open
without a backrest, or enclosed and
filled with cushions. Lissoni's designs
are subtly understated and include
a wide range of seating pieces as well
as interiors and architecture—among
them luxury hotels and resorts.

Robber Baron Table, Studio Job—
Job Smeets and Nynke Tynagel
(Belgium)
2006
Polished, patinated, gilded, and painted
cast bronze

From a suite of five limited-edition
pieces evoking the excesses of
nineteenth- (and twentieth-) century
oligarchs: the base is in the form of
a factory, whose smokestacks spout
a cloud of pollution—symbols of the
industrial society that are sculpted in
the tabletop. Made for Design Miami
2007, in an edition of five.

Do Lo Res Sofa, Ron Arad
(United Kingdom, b. Israel)
2008
Hardwood, flexible polyurethane foam,
removable fabric cover, polypropylene

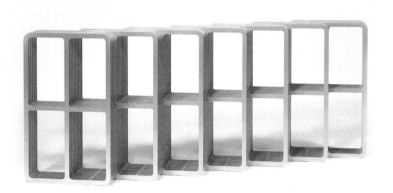

Blo Void 1, Ron Arad
(United Kingdom, b. Israel)
2005
Mirror-polished, anodized, super-plastic
aluminum, woven aluminum mesh

Aluminum is treated like plastic,
inflated into an organic, hollow form.
From Arad's most recent series of works
of design/art in limited editions.

Sequence Bookcase
Pierre Charpin (France)
2008
Metallic varnished aluminum

Made in an edition of eight plus
two artist's proofs and two
prototypes.

Loft Chair, Shelly Shelly
(United States, b. Indonesia)
2008
Walnut

Fly Chair, Patrick Norguet (France)
2009
Coated-metal frame, knitted fabric

Curiosity Kitchen, Alexander Pelikan
(Netherlands)
2010
Mixed ARPA HPL laminates, European
cherry

A witty environment that pays homage
to the convivial social experience of
preparing food, called by designer
Alexander Pelikan a "tasting kitchen."

Alcove Highback Sofa
Ronan & Erwan Bouroullec (France)
2006/2008
Chromed tubular steel, metal, belt
upholstery, fiberglass-reinforced plastic,
polyurethane foam, polyester wool,
microfibers

Slim lines and an ultra-high back
lend a feeling of privacy and enclosure
to a seating group that includes a chair,
a love seat, and sofas of different sizes.

Design as Idea

Some of the most intriguing new furniture designs are as much expressions of artistic impulse as they are functioning objects. They may serve the purpose for which the category was intended—chair, table, storage piece—but they may go beyond it or ignore it altogether. Some function poorly or not at all: chairs that cannot be sat on, cabinets with inconvenient drawers, off-balance tables on variably sized legs. For such pieces, the concept behind the design is as important as the work itself. The viewer is challenged to think about the furniture, perhaps to respond emotionally to it, as design is treated as a language of visual communication. The artist has something to say, which the observer must translate in order to fully appreciate the object—or not.

Montanara, Gaetano Pesce (Italy)
2009
Wood and metal, flexible polyurethane,
digitally printed cotton fabric

Seemingly random, it creates the illusion of
a mountain scene, with snow-capped peaks
and a waterfall seat.

Second Hand Bookcase (Hey Chair, Be a Bookshelf), Maarten Baas (Netherlands, b. Germany)
2006
Wood, polyester resin, polyurethane paint

An assemblage of discarded furniture from secondhand shops, stacked up, then reinforced and hand-painted. Since the original objects vary, no two finished works are exactly alike. Shown in the exhibition European Design Since 1985: Shaping the New Century. Like all of this designer's works, each is made by hand, signed, and numbered. Baas was named Designer of the Year at Design Miami/Basel 2009, and his works have been shown by many major museums. Made in an edition of eight.

Lathe Chair VIII, Sebastian Brajkovic (Netherlands)
2008
Bronze with nitric acid–burned patina,
needle-stitched embroidered fabric

Classic shapes of early-nineteenth-century chairs are extruded and rotated into a whimsical object that retains echoes of its original source. From a series of explorations in exaggerated form begun as Brajkovic's graduation project from Design Academy Eindhoven, this was featured in the Victoria & Albert Museum exhibition Telling Tales. Made in a limited edition of eight plus four artist's proofs, another in the series is in the collection of the Museum of Modern Art.

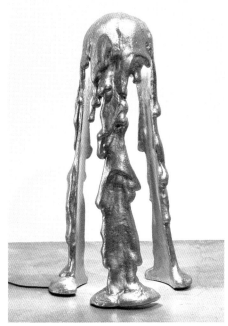

Rococo Armchair, Godspeed (Israel)
2010
Wood scraps, velvet

These conceptually-driven designers create unique works that skip the preliminary sketching phase, starting with the actual assembly of a piece, from waste materials and finishing within a strict one-hour limit. Godspeed is a partnership of Finn Ahlegrenand (b. Sweden) and Joy van Erven (b. Netherlands).

Metal Scum Light, Jerszy Seymour (Canada, b. Germany)
2008
Galvanized metal

Known for his conceptual and experimental projects, Seymour has been featured in many museum exhibitions, including European Design: Shaping the New Century. This piece is from an edition of eight, plus two proofs and one prototype.

Stack, Raw Edges (Israel)
2008
Birch plywood, fiberboard, steel, lacquer

Randomly stacked, or arranged in more conventional fashion, this witty take on conventional storage is in the collection of the Museum of Modern Art. Yael Mer and Shay Alkalay are the partners in Raw Edges.

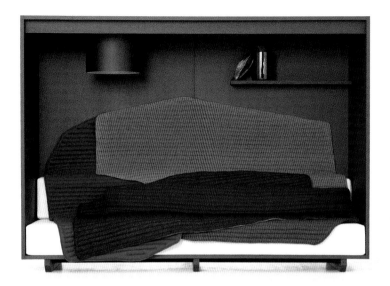

Wrinkle Chair, Shlomo Harush (Israel)
2007
Aluminum
A unique piece.

Sofa, Ronan & Erwan Bouroullec
(France)
2008
Tinted varnished black oak, wool
blankets and cushion, lighting element

Incorporating an overhead light and
storage shelves to create a cocoonlike
living environment, this sofa was in an
edition of eight plus two artist's proofs
and two prototypes.

Crane Lamp, Studio Job—Job Smeets
and Nynke Tynagel
(Belgium/Netherlands)
2010
Cast bronze, light fittings

A centuries-old industrial object scaled
to floor-standing dimensions for a
decorative and practical modern object.
From an edition of six plus one proof.

Taming Technology

Using technology borrowed from other industries—aeronautical, automobile, and film production—these objects meld industrial procedures with aesthetic elements. Designed with computer programs, drawn by motion-capture, fabricated with rapid prototyping, or using other advanced procedures, they represent a category of objects never before possible. In creating these, process, rather than product, is the motivating factor.

Slice Chair, Mathias Bengtsson (Denmark)
2000
Laser-cut aluminum

Early developmental version of design combining technology and handcraft: individual layers are cut by a computer-controlled laser and assembled by hand into a three-dimensional solid form made in an edition of twenty. Other versions were made in wood and cardboard. Shown in the exhibition European Design Since 1985: Shaping the New Century. Bengtsson studied furniture design in Denmark, Switzerland, and London—at the Royal College of Art, under Ron Arad. His designs, mediating between design and art, push the parameters of technology and are in the collections of major museums.

Go Chair, Ross Lovegrove (United Kingdom)
2001
Powder-coated magnesium frame, polycarbonate
or veneer seat

Made possible by advances in computerized design and manufacturing, this ergonomically shaped chair was one of the earliest such pieces designed for mass production and was one of *Time* magazine's "Best Products of 2001." Shown in the exhibition European Design Since 1985: Shaping the New Century. Industrial designer Lovegrove, who calls himself an "evolutionary biologist" and believes that design should be "astonishingly beautiful," is equally focused on technology. In 2005 he received the World Technology Award from CNN.

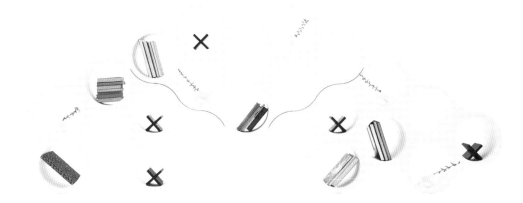

Side Line Table
Philip Michael Wolfson (United States)
2009
Carbon fiber

Made in a limited edition of four.

Drift Concrete, Amanda Levete
(United Kingdom)
2006
Cement, crushed white limestone

A fluid form designed with computer
technology, here translated into an
unexpected material, was originally
executed in high-gloss-finish polyurethane. Levete, an architect, worked for
Richard Rogers and was a partner in
the innovative Future Systems practice
before opening her own office in 2009.

Cloud, Ronan & Erwan Bouroullec
(France)
2004
Polyethylene

A variation on the use of joined
multiples.

Sketch Chair, Front Design (Sweden)
2005
Epoxy resin

Featured in the 2008 exhibition Design
and the Elastic Mind, this technologically
sophisticated design was made using motion-
capture (freehand sketching movements are
digitally recorded on a computer) and rapid
prototyping fabrication. Made in an edition
of three, plus two prototypes, this piece
would have been impossible to fabricate
with conventional manufacturing processes.

Bone Chair, Joris Laarman (Netherlands)
2006
Aluminum

Using software borrowed from the automobile industry, the chair is formed using
structural principles that mimic the natural
growth of bone. The structure is then cast in
aluminum to create an object that is light-
weight and firm, but not static. It was shown
in the exhibition Design and the Elastic Mind;
a related piece, a Bone lounge chair in polyurethane and resin, appeared in the exhibition
European Design Since 1985: Shaping the
New Century.

Impossible Wood, Doshi Levien
(United Kingdom)
2010
Injection-molded liquid wood, tubular metal

Wood fiber, combined with 20% polypropylene, becomes a thermoplastic which is molded
into a shape that contraverts the natural qual-
itites of the material. The design partnership
was esteablished in 2000 by Nipa Doshi and
Jonathan Levien.

Miura Stool, Konstantin Grcic (Germany)
2006
Reinforced polypropylene

Made without fastenings, the entire piece
is injection-molded in a single block.

C1 Chair, Patrick Jouin (France)
2004
Varnished polyester resin

Instead of being assembled from a series of component pieces, this chair was built, bottom to top, as a single unit, using rapid prototyping, now called ALF: Additive Layered Fabrication. It was made in an edition of thirty, with two prototypes.

C2 Chair, Patrick Jouin (France)
2004
Painted epoxy resin

Exploiting the potential of a manufacturing technique previously used to make small models, the skeletal form of this chair is made with rapid prototyping and stereo-lithography. A three-dimensional computer drawing is digitally sliced into layers, which are sent to a machine that builds up layers of material to form complex structures. Jouin, a pioneer in the use of this technology, was recognized in one-man exhibitions at Paris's Centre Pompidou in 2009 and the Museum of Arts and Design in 2010.

Cinderella Table, Jeroen Verhoeven (Netherlands)
2005
Birch and plywood

Traditional design transformed by modern technology: sketches of seventeenth-century tables were fed into a computer to produce a composite drawing translated to three-dimensional form. Then 57 slices of the virtual design were cut by computer, assembled, and finished by hand. Made in an edition of twenty. A marble version was shown in the exhibition Telling Tales. Jeroen Verhoeven, Joep Verhoeven, and Judith de Graauw form collaborative Demakesvan.

Protecting the Planet

Designers' growing awareness of the dictates of Green Design is evidenced by furniture that provides the expected amenities without doing damage to the environment with either the materials used or the method of fabrication. These pieces may use wood from sustainably managed forests, organic fabrics and

fillings, nontoxic dyes, even salvaged wood, shredded magazines, or metal scraps—all employing energy-efficient manufacturing techniques. Since Green Design considers the life cycle of products as well as their fabrication and materials, some designers are even exploring the possibility of furniture that is entirely biodegradable, to be discarded after use. Far from restricting design, the search for sustainability has bred innovation and originality, and much of the resulting furniture is more sensually appealing than severe Modernist design—while mitigating the guilt of living in a wasteful society.

Wrongwoods Cabinet
Richard Wood and Sebastian Wrong
(United Kingdom)
2007
Plywood, timber, paint, lacquer, glass

Tide Chandelier, Stuart Haygarth
(United Kingdom)
2004
Beach-collected man-made debris, monofilament line, MDF, incandescent bulb

Discarded trash gains new meaning in a one-
of-a-kind light fixture made from detritus col-
lected along the coastline in Kent, England.
A miscellaneous assortment of mostly plastic
objects forms a sphere—recalling the moon
on the tides that wash up the debris. Haygarth, trained as a photographer, works with
collections of ordinary objects, transforming
them into functional works that marry craft
and design.

Annie, Reestore (United Kingdom)
2001
Repurposed shopping cart

Making a statement about the importance
of recycling, this seating piece retains the
outline of the originating object.

Brave New World Lamp, Freshwest
(United Kingdom)
2008
Oak frame, cast-iron balancing weights, red
fabric cord

Beginning with the concept of random
construction inspired by Japanese bamboo

scaffolding or children's building toys, the
design team of Marcus Beck and Simon
Macro built this angled lamp of simple materials and without a preconceived form. Each
element of the completed object is pegged
and notched to retain the intricate, random
appearance.

Crate Series No. 8, Jasper Morrison
(United Kingdom)
2008
Powder-coated steel, ash wood,
wax, synthetic webbing

Pixélisée Armchair, Jurgen Bey
(Netherland)
2008
Wood, felt

Made in an edition of six chairs, suggesting a design assembled at random.

Nobody Chair, Komplot (Denmark)
2007
Thermo-pressed PET felt mat

Made without glues, resins, or any reinforcement, this chair is molded from a fully recyclable material whose primary ingredient is discarded soda or water bottles.

Copy and Paste, Sigurdur Gustafsson
(Iceland)
2007
Red, black, white, and natural oak,
polycarbonate

Seemingly assembled from random pieces of wood—a simple form makes a statement about conservation. By Iceland's most prominent architect and furniture designer. Made in an edition of ninety-nine.

V&A Chair #1, Tomás Alonso (Spain)
2009
Reclaimed ash wood, powder-coated steel tubing

Actual boards from Victorian houses were recycled to make this design, an ecologically sensitive offering by Alonso, one of a group of young London designers calling themselves Okay Studio. From an edition of nine.

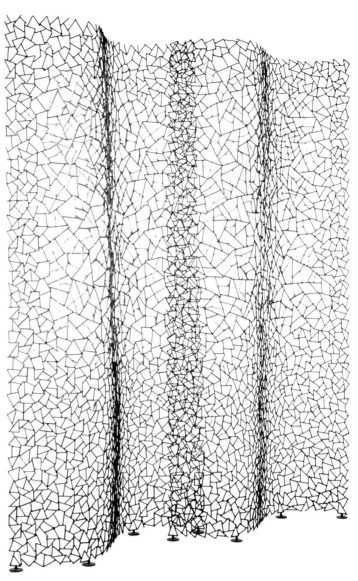

Triangle, Rolu Studio (United States)
2010
Plywood

The simplest geometric form is a
starting point for furniture that is
part sculpture, part functional form.
Rosenlof/Lucas is a Minneapolis-based
studio producing what they refer to as
"found design"—furniture of inexpen-
sive materials in basic forms, inspired
by do-it-yourself books. The firm also
works on landscape architecture and
collaborative public art projects.

Kris Kros Screen, Kenneth Cobonpue
(Philippines)
Hand-tied bamboo pieces, welded
steel frame

An environmentally sensitive material,
from a collection that draws on the
decorative as well as the practical
potential of the materials.

Nature-Driven Design

By recalling anthropomorphic forms, by depicting elements seen in nature, or by making use of materials unaltered by industrial means, these designs recall the attractions of a simpler time, bringing the modern world into comfortable balance with a world preserved mostly in memory. Manifested in forms from nature—twigs, coils, torn and jagged forms, even animals and birds—and sometimes shaped of modern materials, this furniture has an appealing air of old-fashioned nostalgia, recapturing pleasures of the past.

Bouquet, Tokujin Yoshioka (Japan) 2008
Injected polyurethane foam over steel, microfiber fabric, lacquered steel, synthetic rubber
Petal forms of fabric, folded by hand and individually sewn, cover an oval shell to form a seat that suggests a cluster of blossoms. Yoshioka, one of the most original of the current generation of Japanese designers, studied under both Shiro Kuramata and Issey Miyake, and was Designer of the Year at Design Miami/Basel in 2007. He has designed public installations as well as furniture, and his work is in the collections of the Museum of Modern Art, Centre Pompidou, Victoria & Albert Museum, and others.

Leaf Picnic Table and Chairs
René Veenhuizen and Tejo Remy
(Netherlands)
2006
Cut anodized aluminum

Hard-edge material laser-cut into
unusually soft natural forms creates
a sculpture-cum-furniture design,
made in an edition of three.

Collage Illuminated Sculpture
David Wiseman (United States)
2008
Bronze, porcelain, crystal, steel

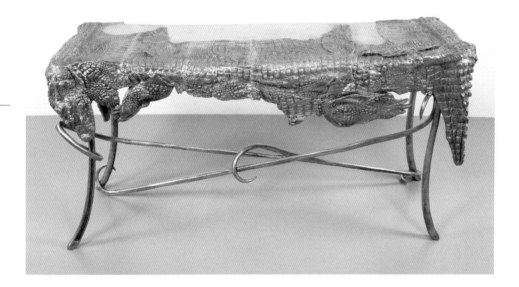

Wings Table, Nigel Coates
(United Kingdom)
2010
Beech wood, aluminum leaf

The hand-carved shape suggests
the layered feathers of eagle wings.
A limited edition of 10 pieces.

Bureau Croc, Claude Lalanne (France)
2007
Bronze

Lalanne uses animal-inspired motifs
here in meticulously worked metal.
Made in a limited edition of eight.

Lantern, Marc Bankowsky (France)
2010
Bronze

Rigid materials sculpted into shapes
suggesting the movement of natural
foliage.

Rocking Beauty, Gudrun Lilja Gunn-
laugsdottir (Iceland)
1991
Water-jet macralon, plywood,
aluminum

Natual motifs formed with machine
techniques, in a limited edition of ten
plus one artist's proof.

Design as Art

Conceived by artists, designers, or architects, this hybrid category of objects includes equal parts furniture and aesthetic experience. These are prototypes, one-off or limited editions, and are not intended for multiple production. In absence of the need to appeal to a broad audience, designers are freer to experi-

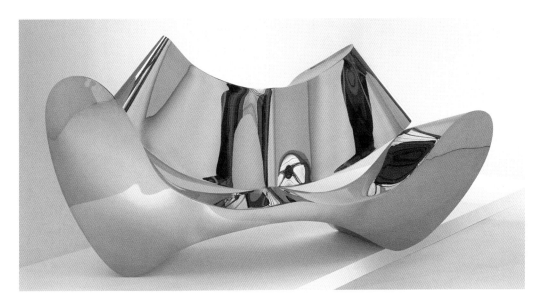

ment or improvise, and the results of their efforts are marketed as collectible in the manner of painting or sculpture. The category is, admittedly, in part a marketing tool that enables designers to gain both status and financial clout, but it expands the parameters and the definitions of what has traditionally been classified as design. Invariably costly, however, this is not good design for everyone; it is for a small and elite market.

D Sofa, Ron Arad
(United Kingdom, b. Israel)
1994
Mirror-polished stainless steel
The contrast of hard material and sensual form in a limited edition of twenty pieces. The seat and the back touch at only three points.

Casino, James Irvine (United Kingdom)
2008
Anodized aluminum

Industrial designer Irvine, who consulted for Olivetti, was also a partner in Sottsass Associati. This work is a limited edition of eight plus two artist's proofs and two prototypes.

Sushi III Chair, Fernando and Humberto Campana (Brazil)
2002
Felt, textiles, plastic, EVA, painted tubular steel

Rolled into concentric rings and set into a tubular steel structure, this is one of a series of designs that suggest Japanese sushi rolls. Made in an edition of thirty-five, with five proofs and three prototypes.

Porcupine Cabinet, Sebastian Errazuri (Chile)
2010
Painted wood, metal and glass

Angular variations in the wood strips are crafted into a functional storage unit that invites the user to play with puzzle-like options for opening its doors. An edition of 12 pieces by an artist whose designs lend unexpected dimension to a familiar material.

Ayana Couch, Hugo Franca (Brazil)
2007
Solid, carved pequi wood

Contextual Craft

Following the standards of the original Arts & Crafts movement, these objects celebrate the hand of the designer-craftsman, providing personalized balance in a depersonalized world. In a category that is increasingly merging into that of design/art, they evidence a new respect for the handcraft tradition. The furniture may be refined and meticulously finished, or deliberately rough-edged and almost primitive. Handcrafted designs, although often costly, reflect inclusiveness and democratic values rather than elitism, along with a much-welcome human touch that softens the hardness of modern life. They echo the mood of a new generation.

 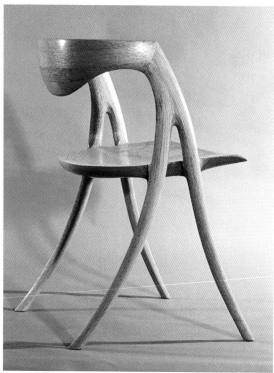

Chair, Kevin Walz (Italy, b. United States)
2008
Ash

A painter turned designer, Walz lives and works in Rome, designing graphics, packaging, and interiors, as well as elegantly spare furniture in natural materials.

Desk Chair, David Ebner
(Italy, b. United States)
2006
Lacewood

Bookhaus with Jack Chairs
Robert Bristow, Pilar Proffitt
(United States)
2010
Barn wood, teak

Nanocrystalline Copper Chair
Max Lamb (United Kingdom)
2008
Electroformed nanocrystalline copper

The aggressively rough surface of
this unique piece is characteristic of
the designs of an artist who bypasses
modern computer technology, using
centuries-old handcraft skills to make
objects that suggest artifacts rather
than newly made art. In his emphasis
on process rather than product, Lamb
has made chairs by pouring molten
metal into sand in his own approach to

traditional sandcasting, or sculpting slabs
of polystyrene into rough-hewn chair forms.
His work has been featured in London's
Design Museum and in design galleries.

Godogan Table, Niels van Eijk and Miriam
van der Lubbe (Netherlands)
2006
American nut

Handmade in Indonesia, this intricately carved
openwork ornament depicts an Indonesian fairy
tale. The table could not have been made in
the West, where comparable craftsmanship no
longer exists. Made in a limited edition of ten.

Desk and Chair, Steven Spiro
(United States)
2000
Walnut, tiger maple, redwood, beech,
wenge, macassar ebony, mother-of-
pearl, trilobites, quartz

Hybride, Ineke Hans (Netherlands)
2006
Polystyrene, pigmented polycast
Made in an edition of five.

Arnold Circus Chair
Martino Gamper (Italy)
2007
Wood, leather
Made in an edition of thirteen
plus three artist's proofs.

Interactive Objects

In furniture of this category, the owner and user becomes a participant in the design process. Each of the objects changes as it is acted upon or as it reacts to the consumer. The user completes the object: folds, hammers, rearranges, bends, or decorates it according to whim or individual taste. The object might also be transformed: chair into table, lamp into lighting fixture, sofa with multiple-section rearrangeable backrests, or lounge chair reshaped by the body occupying it. Such

pieces should not be dismissed as gimmicky; they reflect their designers' attempts to communicate on a more personal level by turning utilization into experience.

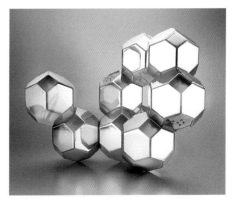

Mosspink Sofa, Kati Meyer-Brühl (Germany)
2008
Natural fabrics or leather, aluminum or wooden legs, angled, triangular, or ball-shaped back form

Offering an easy way to redecorate, this sofa is layered with nature-inspired forms with a practical function: the elements can be removed and rearranged at will to suit the mood, and can be individually replaced when worn. This design won an award at the 2010 International Contemporary Furniture Fair in New York City.

Memory Chair, Tokujin Yoshioka (Japan)
2010
Recycled aluminum fabric over rigid frame

The user participates, and re-participates, in completing the design of a chair, with a dome-shape cover that can be crushed into any desired shape, which is memorized by the material but can be changed at will.

Crystal Light, QisDESIGN (Taiwan)
2010
Polycarbonate, RGB LEDs

The interlocking tetrahedrons can be arranged like a puzzle into several different configurations.

Cabbage Chair, Nendo (Japan, b. Toronto)
2008
Repurposed pleated paper, added resin

The user participates in completing the chair
by peeling back layers to the desired form.
Made without nails, screws, or any structural
foundations. Its pleated paper is a by-product
of fashion designer Issey Miyake's production of pleated fabric. Created in a limited
edition of ten white, ten black, and fourteen
black-and-white. Oki Sato established
Tokyo-based Nendo in 2002. His works have
been acquired by the Montreal Museum of
Fine Arts, the Museum of Modern Art, and
the Musée des Arts décoratifs, among others.

Do Hit Chair, Marijn van der Poll
(Netherlands)
2000
125 mm stainless steel, hammer

Participatory design: the user adjusts
the shape to individual taste with the
hammer.

Walking Table, Wouter Scheublin
(Netherlands)
2006
Wood, metal

This quirky but practical design incorporates
an ingenious human-powered mechanism:
a gentle push or pull of the top converts to
oscillation of the legs that "walk" the table
across the floor.

Unaccustomed Materials

No media are excluded from the possibilities employed in this realm of design—from paper or fabric to all kinds of man-made materials to salvaged fragments culled from the detritus of modern life. Wood shavings or chips, recycled bottles, rubber tires, nautical cording—nothing is too commonplace to consider or to use. In some cases, existing objects are rebuilt, reconfigured, or repurposed to a different function; in others, the materials themselves have been reclaimed and newly utilized.

Table, Arik Levy (Israel)
2007
Glazed bronze
Made in an edition of eight,
plus four artist's proofs.

185

Meltdown Chair, Tom Price
(United Kingdom)
2007
Polypropylene rope

Ordinary nautical rope is coiled into
the desired shape, then heated so that
it "melts" into a finished piece, making
a functional artwork out of commonplace material.

Sharpei, Massimiliano Adami (Italy)
2008
Beechwood and fabric

REINVENTING MODERNISM: THE TWENTY-FIRST CENTURY

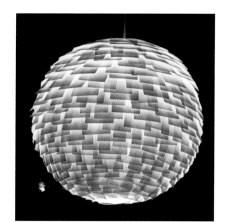

Paperless Chandelier, JAM
(United Kingdom)
2003
Paper clips, acrylic

More than the sum of its parts, an
elegant and unique object assembled
from the simplest, taken-for-granted
elements.

Birdie Chandelier, Ingo Maurer
(Germany)
2002
Metal, goose-feather wings, lightbulbs

Ordinary incandescent bulbs (with
halogen innards) seem to literally take
flight in a whimsical design of curlicued
metal wire punctuated by pairs of real
feathers.

Post-It Lamp, Godspeed (Israel)
2009
Post-Its with Asian paper lamp as frame

Moving directly from concept to
fabrication, and bypassing the sketching phase, this design turns a desktop
essential into a design medium.

Large Optical Chandelier
Stuart Haygarth (United Kingdom)
2007
Glass and plastic prescription eyeglass
lenses, metal, monofilament line,
sprayed MDF

Witch Chair, Tord Boontje
(Netherland)
2002
Hardwood, flame-retardant polyurethane foam, leather

A modern tweaking of Victoriana, with
a faintly traditional form enveloped
in overlapping scale-like rectangles of
black leather.

Quark 20, Emmanuel Babled (France)
2010
Plexiglas

Made in a limited series, seven pieces
in each shape, with a sculptural form
creating the effect of flowing clear
liquid.

FLIGHTS OF FANTASY

Neither precisely design/art nor exactly conceptual design, this category of objects seems intended for nothing so much as the amusement of the maker—and the user. Furniture in such cases, like pictures, can be used to tell a story, relating the objects to human experience. It might recall childhood imaginings or fairy tales, evoking youthful pleasures in an adult world.

Seesaw, Louise Campbell (Denmark)
2003
Wood, polyurethane foam, fabric
Campbell's design combines wit and practicality—comfortable seating that requires teamwork, since it requires two occupants to find their proper balance.

Dog House, Michael Young
(United Kingdom)
2001
Rotational-molded polyethylene, underframe in stainless steel rod

Blossom Chandelier, Tord Boontje
(Netherlands)
2002
Enameled steel, clear crystal, crystal AB coating
A version of this piece was in the exhibition European Design Since 1985: Shaping the New Century. Boontje draws inspiration from both art and craft in lighting designs that are delicate and yet technically sophisticated, evolving from his early applications of found materials and objects. Trained at Eindhoven and London's Royal College of Art, he now works and teaches in London.

Mixed Banquete Chair, Fernando and Humberto Campana (Brazil)
ca. 2003
Stuffed animals, brushed tubular steel

A commentary on childhood's favorite things, one of several variations of a not-for-actual-sitting chair made individually in numbered editions, this one an edition of 150 with five proofs and three prototypes. Other variations used stuffed alligators, pandas, or sharks and dolphins.

Quasimodo Cabinet, Mattia Bonetti (France, b. Switzerland)
2009
Patinated resin, tinted wood, patinated wrought iron

Made in an edition of eight. Bonetti juxtaposes divergent materials to create an object that is at once refined and rough-hewn.

Family Lamp, Atelier van Lieshout
(Netherlands)
2007
Patinated bronze

Anthropomorphism in a witty design with
personality from the studio established in
Rotterdam by Joep van Lieshout in 1995.
Made in a limited edition of twelve.

Mangrove Chair, Eiji Shibata (Japan)
2007
Powder-coated steel

A continuous ribbon of springy steel flows
seamlessly from seat to back and base.

Myto, Cantilever Chair, Konstantin Grcic
(Germany)
2008
Ultradur® high-speed plastic

Sparkling Chair, Marcel Wanders
(Netherlands)
2010
Blow-molded polystyrene

The chair was made by a process customarily
used for making bottles, as suggested by the
transparent form and rounded-end legs.

Cartoon, Gam Fratesi Studio (Denmark)
2008
Solid oak, braided elastic ribbons,
high-resilience foam

Table Basse Anneaux, Ingrid Donat
(France)
2008
Bronze

Made in an edition of eight.

SUMMING UP

The landscape of twenty-first-century design has too many hills and valleys, too many slippery slopes, to permit the charting of a clear path to the future. Our perspective is continually distorted by changes in the literal and figurative climate, by economic and political shifts, and by the warp-speed transformative technology that will ultimately shape the decades to come.

There is, however, one truism we can acknowledge. Nothing will be as it was before; with the tools and materi-

als available to designers today, it is unlikely that any single style will ever dominate in the way in which one marked most periods in the past. That is precisely why we should probably abandon efforts to formulate or reformulate a strict definition of Modernism, or even of design. Both are moving targets, as they should be. It might be wiser to simply accept the fact that whatever is being designed today, no matter how radical its components or configuration, will metamorphose into the Modernism that defines the twenty-first century.

One-Shot.mgx Stool, Patrick Jouin (France)
2006
Polyamide
Like an umbrella, this space-age stool opens or closes by pressing or pulling the center handle. It is created in a single three-dimensional stereolithographic printing operation. It is in the collections of the Museum of Modern Art and the Smithsonian Cooper-Hewitt National Design Museum.

A Line, Anya Sebton (Sweden)
2004
Extruded aluminum beam, hardwood frame, injection-molded foam, fabric

Parts of a Rainbow, Christian Flindt (Denmark)
2005
Repsol glass

Ingenious variation on the conventional stacking
chair, this set of ten colorful seats stacks laterally
to form a color-shifting, light-reflecting decorative
treatment when not in use.

U = UPPER   L = LOWER   C = CENTER   L = LEFT   R = RIGHT

1

Courtesy of Rago Arts and Auction Center

2

Producer: One Off
H 51", W 36", D 54" (129.5 x 91.4 x 137.2 cm)
Courtesy of Friedman Benda

5

Producer: Ingo Maurer GmbH
H 47 1/4", W 47 1/4" (119.9 x 119.9 cm)
Courtesy of Ingo Maurer GmbH

6

L Producer: Fredericia
H 33", W 19 1/2", D 21" (83.5 x 49.5 x 53 cm)
Courtesy of Fredericia
C Producer: Cappellini
H 31 1/2", W 20", D 15" (80 x 50.8 x 38.1 cm)
Courtesy of Cappellini
R Producer: Moooi
H 43", W 28 1/3", D 28 1/3" (110 x 72 x 72 cm)
Courtesy of Moooi

9

L Producer: Moooi
H 32 3/4", W 24 1/2", D 25 1/4" (83 x 62 x 64 cm)
Courtesy of Moooi
R Producer: Porro
H 30", W 19 3/4", D 17 3/4" (76 x 50 x 45 cm)
Courtesy of Porro

10

UL Producer: Kartell, Habitat Division
H 22 1/2", W 28 1/2", H 22 1/2" (57.2 x 72.4 x 57.2 cm)
Courtesy of Wright 20
LL H 21", W 29", D 15" (53.3 x 73.7 x 38.1 cm)
Courtesy of Wright 20
UC D 29 1/4" (74.3 cm)
Courtesy of Phillips de Pury & Company
LC Producer: Hansen & Sorensen
H 26 3/4", W 33 1/2", D 30" (68 x 85 x 76.2 cm)
Courtesy of Hansen & Sorensen
UR Producer: Rosenthal
H 24 1/2", W 266", D 35" (62.2 x 675.6 x 88.9 cm)
Courtesy of Wright 20
LR Producer: B & B Italia
H 60 1/4", W 40 1/4", D 32 3/4" (153 x 102 x 83 cm)
Courtesy of B & B Italia

11

Producer: Magis
H 74 2/5", DIA 26 3/5" (189 x 67.5 dia cm)
Courtesy of Magis

12

L Producer: Stilnovo
H 36", DIA 30 1/2" (91.4 x 77.5 dia cm)
Courtesy of Wright 20
R Producer: Disform
H 27 3/4", W 21 1/2", D 18" (70.5 x 54.6 x 45.7 cm
Courtesy of Rago Arts and Auction Center

13

Producer: New City Editions
H 32", W 28", D 83" (81.3 x 71.1 x 210.8 cm)
Courtesy of Wright 20

14

Producer: Magis
H 32 1/3", W 21 3/4", D 23 1/4" (82 x 55.1 58.9 cm)
Courtesy of Magis
R Producer: Källemo
H 15 3/4", DIA 25 3/4" (40 x 65 dia cm)
Courtesy of Källemo

16

Producer: Droog/DMD
H 30", W 50", D 50" (76.2 x 127 x 127 cm)
Courtesy of Droog

17

Producer: Vitra
H 32 1/2", W 19 1/4", D 23" (83 x 49 x 58 cm)
Courtesy of Wright 20

18

L Producer: Hove Mobler
H 41", W 29", D 34" (104.1 x 73.7 x 86.4 cm)
Courtesy of Wright 20
R Producer: Artifort
H 27 1/2", W 32", D 34" (69.9 x 81.3 x 86.4 cm)
Courtesy of Wright 20

19

Producer: Dunbar
H 27 1/2", W 81", D 28" (69.9 x 205.7 x 71.1 cm)
Courtesy of Wright 20

20

L H 35 1/2", W 21", D 21" (90.2 x 53.3 x 53.3 cm)
Courtesy of Wright 20
R Producer: Arredoluce
H 65", W 35", D 35" (165.1 x 88.9 x 88.9 cm)
Courtesy of Wright 20

21

Producer: B & B Italia
H 41", W 43 1/2", D 48" (104.1 x 110.5 x 121.9 cm)
Courtesy of Wright 20

22

Producer: Herman Miller
H 28 1/2", W 76", D 17" (72.4 x 193 x 43.2 cm)
Courtesy of Rago Arts and Auction Center

23

L Producer: Herman Miller
H 33", W 40", D 60" (83.8 x 101.6 x 152.4 cm)
Courtesy of Wright 20
R Producer: Erik Jørgensen
H 35 1/2", W 39", D 39" (90 x 99 x 99 cm)
Courtesy of Erik Jørgensen

24

L Producer: Lavernes
H 37 1/2", DIA 14" (95.3 x 35.6 dia cm)
Courtesy of Wright 20
UC Producer: Haimi
H 36 1/2", W 28 1/2", D 30" (92.7 x 72.4 x 76.2 cm)
Image Courtesy of Wright 20
LC Producer: Plus-linje
H 32", W 24", D 24" (81.3 x 61 x 61 cm)
Courtesy of Wright 20
LR Producer: Swedese
H 39", W 28", D 29" (99 x 71.1 x 73.7 cm)
Courtesy of Wright 20

25

U Producer: Poltranova
H 23 1/2", W 102", D 102" (59.7 x 259 x 259 cm)
Courtesy of Wright 20
L Producer: Knoll International
H 28 1/2", W 65", D 55" (72.4 x 165.1 x 139.7 cm)
Courtesy of Wright 20

26

Producer: Vitra
H 32 3/4" (83.2 cm)
Courtesy of Phillips de Pury & Company

27

L H 17 1/2", DIA 47" (44.5 x 119.4 dia cm)
Courtesy of Wright 20
R Producer: Artifort
H 25 3/4", W 29 1/2", D 29" (65.4 x 74.9 x 73.7 cm)
Courtesy of Wright 20

28

H 12 3/4", W 40", D 40" (32.4 x 101.6 x 101.6 cm)
Courtesy of Wright 20

29

L Producer: Design Steel
H 32", W 28 1/2", D 23" (81.3 x 72.4 x 58.4 cm)
Courtesy of Phillips de Pury & Company

R Producer: Skipper
H 16", W 39 1/2", D 24 1/2" (40.6 x 100.3 x 62.2 cm)
Courtesy of Wright 20

30
Producer: Emeco
H 34", W 15 1/2", D 19 1/2" (86 x 39 x 50 cm)
Courtesy of Emeco
Photograph by Mikio Sekita

31
L Producer: Ivan Schlecter
H 25", W 32 1/2", D 27" (63.5 x 82.6 x 68.6 cm)
Courtesy of Wright 20
R Producer: Compagnie d'Esthetique Industrielle (C.E.I.)
H 49 1/2", W 41", D 22" (125.7 x 104.1 x 55.9 cm)
Courtesy of Wright 20

32
L Producer: Knoll International
H 14", W 44", D 44" (35.5 x 111.8 x 111.8 cm)
Courtesy of Wright 20
R Producer: Edison Price, Inc
H 41 1/2", DIA 25" (105.4 x 63.5 dia cm)
Courtesy of Wright 20

33
Producer: Fritz Hansen
H 33 1/2", W 60", D 26" (85.1 x 152.4 x 66 cm)
Courtesy of Phillips de Pury & Company

34
UL Producer: Piiroinen
H 26", W 17 3/4", D 20 7/8" (66 x 45.1 x 53.1 cm)
Courtesy of Piiroinen
LL H 80", W 37" (203.2 x 94 cm)
Courtesy of Wright 20
LC Producer: Cassina
H 39 1/2", W 18", D 25" (100.3 x 45.7 x 63.5 cm)
Courtesy of Phillips de Pury & Company
UR **Courtesy of Rago Arts and Auction Center**
LR H 22", W 20 1/2", D 20" (55.9 x 52.1 x 50.8 cm)
Courtesy of Wright 20

35
L Producer: Umbra
H 34", W 24", D 24" (86 x 61 x 61 cm)
Courtesy of Umbra
R Producer: Flexform
H 24", W 24", D 44" (61 x 61 x 111.8 cm)
Courtesy of Wright 20

36
L Producer: Studio 65
H 25 1/2", W 144", D 50" (64.8 x 365.8 x 127 cm)
Courtesy of Wright 20
R H 37", W 20", D 20" (94 x 50.8 x 50.8 cm)
Courtesy of Wright 20

37
Producer: Gavina for Knoll International
H 61", W 80", D 25" (155 x 203.2 x 63.5 cm)
Courtesy of Wright 20

38
L Producer: Airborne International
H 25", W 68", D 24" (64 x 173 x 61 cm)
Courtesy of Wright 20
R Producer: Akari
H 76", W 19", D 19" (193 x 48.3 x 48.3 cm)
Courtesy of Wright 20

39
L Producer: Poltrona Moleca
H 29", W 46", D 37" (73.7 x 116.9 x 94 cm)
Courtesy of Wright 20
R H 20" (50.8 cm)
Courtesy of Phillips de Pury & Company

40
U Producer: Cappellini
H 20", W 72", D 29" (50.8 x 182.9 x 73.7 cm)
Courtesy of Wright 20
L H 17", W 20", D 11 1/2" (43.2 x 50.8 x 29.2 cm)
Courtesy of Wright 20

41
L Producer: Flos
H 98 1/2", W 13", D 78 1/2" (250.2 x 33 x 199.4 cm)
Courtesy of Wright 20
R Producer: Avarte
H 28 1/3", W 37 2/5", D 33" (72 x 96 x 83.5 cm)
Courtesy of Avarte

42
L Producer: Artemide
W 68", DIA 3" (172.7 x 7.6 dia cm)
Courtesy of Wright 20
R Producer: HAG
H 17 1/4", W 22 3/4", D 12" (44 x 58 x 30 cm)
Courtesy of HAG

43
Producer: Ugine-Gueugnon
H 12 1/2", W 118", D 39 1/4" (31.8 x 299.7 x 99.7 cm)
Courtesy of Phillips de Pury & Company
Image Courtesy of Moderne Gallery
Photo by M.J. Joniec

44
L Producer: Poltronova
Chair: H 30", W 29", D 51 1/2"; Ottoman: H 12". Chair: (76.2 x 73.7 x 130.8 cm); Ottoman: (30.5 cm)
Courtesy of Phillips de Pury & Company
R Producer: Arteluce
Courtesy of Rago Arts and Auction Center

45
L H 12", W 20 1/2" (30.5 x 52.1 cm)
Courtesy of Rago Arts and Auction Center
LR Producer: Anonima Castelli
H 29 1/2", W" 18 1/2", D 19" (75 x 47 x 48 cm)
Courtesy of Wright 20

46
L Producer: Kill International
H 32 1/2", W 56", D 28 3/4" (82.6 x 142.2 x 73 cm)
Courtesy of Wright 20
R Producer: Artek
Courtesy of Artek

47
L H 48", W 37", D 25" (121.9 x 94 x 63.5 cm)
Courtesy of Wright 20
R H 60", W 23", D 46" (152.4 x 58.4 x 116.8 cm)
Courtesy of Wright 20

48
Producer: De Sede
H 37", W 157 1/2", D 29 1/2" (94 x 400.1 x 74.9 cm)
Courtesy of Phillips de Pury & Company

49
L Producer: Lammhults
H 30", W 18 1/2", D 19 3/8" (75.9 x 47 x 49 cm)
Courtesy of Lammhults
R Producer: E. Kold Christensen
H 25 1/2", DIA 55 1/4" (extendable to DIA 85") (64.8, 140.3 dia cm)
Courtesy of R 20th Century Design

50
Producer: Beylerian/Kartell
H 28", W 16 1/2", D 19 1/4" (71.1 x 41.9 x 48.9 cm)
Courtesy of Phillips de Pury & Company

51
L Producer: Studio Alchimia
H 39 3/8" (100 cm)
Courtesy of Phillips de Pury & Company
UC Producer: Northern Plastics United States
H 22", W 37 1/2", D 35" (55.9 x 95.3 x 88.9 cm)
Courtesy of Wright 20
LC Producer: Lammhults
H 28", W 19", D 19" (71 x 48 x 48 cm)
Courtesy of Lammhults
R Producer: Cappellini
H 72", W 27", D 19 3/4" (182.9 x 68.6 x 50.2 cm)
Courtesy of Cappellini

52
UL H 18", W 23 1/2", D 23 1/2" (45.7 x 59.7 x 59.7 cm)
Courtesy of Wright 20
LL H 11", W 47 1/2", D 23 1/2" (27.9 x 120.7 x 59.7 cm)
Courtesy of Wright 20
R Producer: Vitra
H 29 1/2", W 25 1/2", D 25 1/2" (74.9 x 64.8 x 64.8 cm)
Courtesy of Vitra
Photograph by Marc Eggimann

53
L Producer: Lammhults
H 41 3/4"/47 1/4", W 27 3/4", D 27 3/4" (106/120 x 70.5 x 70.5 cm)
Courtesy of Lammhults
R H 47", W 120", D 44" (119.4 x 304.8 x 111.8 cm)
Courtesy of Rago Arts and Auction Center

54
L Producer: B & B Italia
H 27 1/2", W 84 1/2", D 46" (70 x 215 x 117 cm)
Courtesy of B & B Italia
R Producer: Cassina
H 28 1/3"-39 1/2", W 65 1/3", D 37 1/2" (72-100 x 166 x 95.3 cm)
Courtesy of Cassina

55
Producer: Galerie Mikro
H 29 3/4" (75.6 cm)
Courtesy of J. Lohmann Gallery

58
UL Producer: Erik Jørgensen
H 36 1/2", W 31", D 34" (92.7 x 78.7 x 86.4 cm)
Courtesy of Erik Jørgesen
LL H 19 1/2", DIA 18" (49.5 x 45.7 dia cm)
Courtesy of Wright 20
UC Producer: Memphis-Milano
H 49 1/4", W 45 1/4", D 43 1/4" (125 x 115 x 110 cm)
Courtesy of Memphis-Milano

LC Producer: Stilnovo
H 32", DIA 42" (81.3,106.7 dia cm)
Courtesy of Wright 20
UR Producer: Laverne International
H 23 1/2", W 31", D 27" (59.7 x 78.7 x 68.6 cm)
Courtesy of Phillips de Pury & Company

59
L Producer: Cassina
H 46", W 41", D 34" (117 x 104 x 86 cm)
Courtesy of Wright 20
C Producer: E. Kold Christensen
H 26 1/2", W 25 1/4", D 20 1/2" (67.3 x 64.1 x 52 cm)
Courtesy of Wright 20
R Producer: Knoll
H 30 1/2", W 36", D 27" (77.5 x 91.4 x 68.6 cm)
Courtesy of Wright 20

60
U Producer: Tendo Brasiliera
H 31", W 70", D 23 7/8" (78.7 x 177.8 x 60.6 cm)
Courtesy of Phillips de Pury & Company
L Producer: Gavina
H 27 1/2", W 59", D 43 1/3" (69.9 x 149.9 x 110 cm)
Courtesy of R 20th Century Design

61
L Producer: Airbourne
H 23 1/2", W 58", D 24" (59.7 x 147.3 x 61 cm)
Courtesy of Phillips de Pury & Company
R **Courtesy of Rago Arts and Auction Center**

62
Producer: Arredoluce
H 24" (61 cm)
Courtesy of Phillips de Pury & Company

63
UL Producer: Stokke
H 31-32 3/4", W 30", D 29 1/2"" (79-83 x 75 x 76 cm)
Courtesy of Stokke
LL Producer: Verre Lumiere
H 22", DIA 44" (55.9 x 111.8 dia cm)
Courtesy of Wright 20
UR H 33 1/2", W 26", D 38" (85.1 x 66 x 96.5 cm)
Courtesy of Wright 20
LR Producer: New Lamp
H 20", W 20", D 20" (50.8 x 50.8 x 50.8 cm)
Courtesy of Wright 20

64
U Producer: Pod
H 35", W 60", D 25" (88.9 x 152.4 x 63.5 cm)
Courtesy of Phillips de Pury & Company
L H 34 1/2", W 58 1/2", D 16" (87.6 x 148.6 x 40.6 cm)
Courtesy of Rago Arts and Auction Center

67
L Producer: Cappellini
H 40 1/4", W 19 3/4", D 16 1/2" (102.2 x 50.2 x 41.9 cm)
Courtesy of Cappellini
R Producer: Cappellini
H 28 1/4", W 53 1/4", D 27 1/2" (71.8 x 135.3 x 69.9 cm)
Courtesy of Cappellini

68
UL Producer: Kappa
H 14 3/4", W 75", D 27 1/2" (37.5 x 190.5 x 69.9 cm)

CL H 30 3/4", W 83 1/4", D 36" (78.1 x 211.5 x 91.4 cm)
Courtesy of Wright 20
LL H 15", W 80", D 35" (38.1 x 203.2 x 88.9 cm)
Courtesy of Wright 20
CR Producer: Magis
H 32 1/3", W 21 3/4", D 23 1/4" (82 x 55.1 x 58.9 cm)
Courtesy of Magis

69
U Producer: Artifort
H 29 1/8", W 75 5/8", D 33 1/8" (73.9 x 192 x 84.1 cm)
Courtesy of Artifort
L Producer: Kagan-Dreyfuss Inc.
H 29", W 96", D 32" (73.7 x 243.8 x 81.3 cm)
Courtesy of Wright 20

70
Producer: Edra
H 39", W 161", D 33" (99.1 x 408.9 x 83.8 cm)
Courtesy of Wright 20

71
U Producer: Knoll
Chair: H 33", W 32", D 32"; Ottoman: H 14", W 24", D 24"; Chair: (83.8 x 81.3 x 81.3 cm); Ottoman: (35.6 x 61 x 61 cm)
Courtesy of Wright 20
L Producer: Poltranova
4 Seater Sofa: W 106 1/4" (269.9 cm)
Courtesy of Vignelli Associates

72
UL Producer: Tecno
H 29 1/4", W 86 1/2", D 39 1/2" (74.3 x 219.7 x 100.3 cm)
Courtesy of Wright 20
R Producer: Knoll International
H 38 1/2", W 23", D 22" (97.8 x 58.4 x 55.9 cm)
Courtesy of Wright 20

73
U Producer: Knoll International
H 27 1/2", W 21", D 20" (69.9 x 53.3 x 50.8 cm)
Courtesy of Wright 20
L Producer: Martinelli Luce
H 28", DIA 20" (71.1, 50.8 dia cm)
Courtesy of Wright 20

75
Courtesy of Rago Arts and Auction Center

76
UL Producer: Easy Edges Inc.
H 25", W 23 1/2", D 42" (63.5 x 59.7 x 106.7 cm)
Courtesy of Wright 20
UR Producer: Top System
H 19 3/4", W 14", D 21" (50.2 x 35.6 x 53.3 cm)
Courtesy of Wright 20
L Producer: De Sede
(Single Piece) H 27 1/2", W 61 1/2", D 27 1/2" (69.9 x 156.2 x 69.9 cm)
Courtesy of De Sede

77
LR Producer: Rosenthal Studio Line
H 13", W 9" (33 x 22.9 cm)
Courtesy of J. Lohmann Gallery
LL H 19", W 21", D 24" (48.3 x 53.3 x 61 cm)
Courtesy of R 20th Century Design
Photograph by Sherry Griffin
U H 29 1/2", W 54", D 23" (74.9 x 137.2 x 58.4 cm)
Courtesy of Phillips de Pury & Company

79
L Producer: Cappellini
H 32 1/2", W 25 1/2", D 42" (82.6 x 64.8 x 106.7 cm)
Courtesy of Cappellini
R Producer: Thayer Coggin, Inc.
H 24", W 84", D 32" (61 x 213 x 81 cm)
Courtesy of Wright 20

80
L H 32 1/2", W 72", D 18" (83 x 183 x 46 cm)
Courtesy of Wright 20
R Producer: Cassina
H 38", W 56", D 29" (96.5 x 142.2 x 73.7 cm)
Courtesy of Wright 20

81
UR Producer: Fredericia
H 38 1/2", W 59", D 27 1/2" (98 x 150 x 70 cm)
Courtesy of Fredericia
UL H 29 1/2", W 31", D 24" (74.9 x 78.7 x 61 cm)
Courtesy of Wright 20

83
L Producer: Poggi
H 49 1/4", W 19 3/4", D 17" (125 x 50 x 43 cm)
Courtesy of Nilufar
R Producer: Cassina
H 26 1/2", W 70", D 38" (67.3 x 177.8 x 96.5 cm)
Courtesy of Wright 20

84
UL Producer: Gufram
H 36", W 83", D 32" (91.4 x 210.8 x 81.3 cm)
Courtesy of Wright 20
LL Producer: Dall' Oca
H 27 1/2", W 84", D 41" (69.9 x 213.4 x 104.1 cm)
Courtesy of Wright 20
UR Producer: Nucleo for Sormani
H 31", W 45", D 45" (78.7 x 114.3 x 114.3 cm)
Courtesy of Wright 20
LR Producer: Cassina
H 31", W 26 1/2", D 23" (78.7 x 67.3 x 58.4 cm)
Courtesy of Wright 20

85
U Producer: Poltranova
H 36", W 42", D 62" (91.4 x 106.7 x 157.5 cm)
Courtesy of Wright 20
L Producer: Artemide
H 52", W 14", D 14" (132.1 x 35.6 x 35.6 cm)
Courtesy of Wright 20

86
L H 41 3/4", W 42 1/8", D 41 3/4" (106 x 107.1 x 106 cm)
Courtesy of Cappellini
R Producer: Arteluce
H 9 3/4", W 3 3/4" (24.8 x 9.5 cm)
Courtesy of Wright 20

87
UL Producer: Stendig
H 28 1/4", W 28 3/4", D 36" (71.8 x 73 x 91.4 cm)
Courtesy of Wright 20
LL Producer: Bracciodiferro
H 30", W 77", 47 1/4" (76.2 x 195.6 x 120 cm)
Courtesy of Phillips de Pury & Company
UR Producer: Fontana Arte
H 13", W 60", D 60" (33 x 152.4 x 152.4 cm)
Courtesy of Rago Arts and Auction Center
LR Producer: Rosenthal Studio-Line
H 29", W 127 1/2", D 100" (73.7 x 323.9 x 254 cm)
Courtesy of Wright 20

L H 44", W 15 1/2", D 20" (111.8 x 39.4 x 50.8 cm)
Courtesy of Rago Arts and Auction Center
R H 29 1/2" x W 64"
Courtesy of Rago Arts and Auction Center

90

L H 33", W 24", D 86" (84 x 61 x 218.4 cm)
Courtesy of Rago Arts and Auction Center
R H 46 1/2", W 27 1/2", D 44" (118.1 x 69.9 x 111.8 cm)
Courtesy of Wright 20

91

L **Courtesy of Rago Arts and Auction Center**
R **Courtesy of Rago Arts and Auction Center**

92

L **Courtesy of Moderne Gallery**
Photograph by M.J. Joniec
R H 32 1/2", W 80 3/4", H 30 1/4" (82.6 x 205.1 x 76.8 cm)
Courtesy of Sebastian + Barquet

93

L **Courtesy of Rago Arts and Auction Center**
UR H 33", DIA 42" (83.8 x 106.7 dia cm)
Courtesy of Phillips de Pury & Company
CR H 29 1/2", D 81 1/2" (74.9 x 207 cm)
Courtesy of R 20th Century Design
LR H 17 1/2", W 10", DIO" (44.5 x 25.4 x 25.4 cm)
Courtesy of Rago Arts and Auction Center

95

L Producer: Alias Design
H 38", W 39", D 44" (96.5 x 99.1 x 111.8 cm)
Courtesy of Wright 20
R Producer: Gufram
H 26 1/2", W 44", D 44" (67.3 x 111.8 x 111.8 cm)
Courtesy of Wright 20

96

UL Producer: Ishimaru Co., Ltd.
H 28", W 59", D 32 1/4" (71.1 x 149.9 x 81.9 cm)
Courtesy of Wright 20
LL Producer: Poltranova
H 38 1/5", W 82 3/4", D 36 3/5" (97 x 210 x 93 cm)
Courtesy of Quittenbaum Art Auctions
R Producer: Knoll International
H 33 1/4", W 23 1/2", D 23 1/2" (84.5 x 59.7 x 59.7 cm)
Courtesy of Wright 20

97

L Producer: Memphis
H 35", W 26", D 19" (88.9 x 66 x 48.3 cm)
Courtesy of Wright 20

R Producer: Cassina
H 48", W 88", D 37" (121.9 x 223.5 x 94 cm)
Courtesy of Wright 20

98

L **Courtesy of Rago Arts and Auction Center**
R Producer: Venini
H 38", W 15 1/2", D 15 1/2" (96.5 x 39.4 x 39.4 cm)
Courtesy of Wright 20

99

L Producer: Cassina
H 40 1/4", W 32 3/4", D 35 1/3"-53" (102 x 83 x 90-135 cm)
Courtesy of Cassina
R Producer: UP & UP for Memphis
H 16", DIA 51 1/4" (40.6 x 130.2 dia cm)
Courtesy of Phillips de Pury & Company

100

L Producer: Zabro
H 88", W 71 3/4", D 37" (223.5 x 182.2 x 94 cm)
Courtesy of Phillips de Pury & Company
R **Courtesy of Rago Arts and Auction Center**

101

L Producer: Memphis
H 77", W 75", D 16" (195.6 x 190.5 x 40.6 cm)
Courtesy of Rago Arts and Auction Center
R Producer: Driade Aleph
H 26 1/4", W 24", D 31" (66.7 x 61 x 78.7 cm)
Courtesy of Phillips de Pury & Company

102

U Producer: Cappellini
H 50", W 23", D 22" (127 x 58 x 56 cm)
Courtesy of Wright 20
L H 20 1/2", W 20 3/4", D 24" (52.1 x 52.7 x 61 cm)
Courtesy of Wright 20

103

L **Courtesy of Moderne Gallery**
Photograph by M.J. Joniec
UR Producer: Studio Alchimia
H 55" (139.7 cm)
Courtesy of Phillips de Pury & Company
LR Producer: Gemini G.E.L.
H 22", W 39 1/2", D 37" (55.9 x 100.3 x 94 cm)
Courtesy of Wright 20

105

L Producer: Arredoluce
H 79", DIA 12 3/4" (200.7 x 32.4 dia cm)
Courtesy of Wright 20
R Producer: Magis
H 37 1/2", W 78 3/4", D 26 7/8" (95.3 x 200 x 68.1 cm)
Courtesy of Magis

106

UL Producer: Multiples, Inc./Marian Goodman Gallery
H 16", W 48", D 48" (40.6 x 121.9 x 121.9 cm)
Courtesy of Wright 20
UR H 14 1/2", W 14 1/2", D 27" (36.8 x 36.8 x 68.6 cm)
Courtesy of Wright 20
L Producer: Fredericia
W 36", L 75" (extendable to 120") (91 x 190.5/305 cm)
Courtesy of Fredericia

107

L H 48", W 16", D 23" (121.9 x 40.6 x 58.4 cm)
Courtesy of Wright 20
R Producer: Danny Lane Studio
H 34 4/5", W 15", D 23 1/5" (88.5 x 38 x 59 cm)
Courtesy of Quittenbaum Art Auctions

108

L Producer: One Off
H 26", W 26", D 35" (66 x 66 x 89 cm)
Courtesy of R 20th Century Design

R Producer: Källemo
H 29", W 28", D 37" (73.7 x 71.1 x 94 cm)
Courtesy of Wright 20

109

L Producer: Néotù
H 46" (116.8 cm)
Courtesy of Phillips de Pury & Company
R H 21", W 24", D 26" (53.3 x 61 x 66 cm)
Courtesy of Wright 20

110

L Producer: Droog/DMD
H 47 1/4", W 43 1/3", D 23 1/2" (variable) (120 x 110 x 60 cm)
Courtesy of Droog
Photograph by Gerard van Hees
R H 5 1/2", W 6 3/4", D 7 1/2" (14 x 17.1 x 19.1 cm)
Courtesy of Rago Arts and Auction Center

111

H 21 1/2", W 97", D 20" (54.6 x 247 x 51 cm)
Courtesy of Rago Arts and Auction Center

112

L Producer: Vitra Editions
H 30", W 37", D 33" (76.2 x 94 x 83.8 cm)
Courtesy of Wright 20
UR Producer: DMD/Droog Designs
H 35", DIA 24" (88.9 x 61 cm)
Courtesy of Wright 20
LR H 54 3/4", W 31 1/2", D 27 1/2" (139 x 80 x 70 cm)
Courtesy of Paul Kasmin Gallery

113

L Producer: Droog/DMD
H 39 1/2", W 23 1/2", D 23 1/2" (100 x 60 x 60 cm)
Courtesy of Droog
Photograph by Gerard van Hees
R H 35", W 21 1/2", D 27" (89 x 54.6 x 68.6 cm)
Courtesy of Rago Arts and Auction Center

114

Producer: SCP Furniture
H 46", W 78", D 34" (116.8 x 198.1 x 86.4 cm)
Courtesy of Phillips de Pury & Company

115

L H 26", W 32", D 27" (66 x 81.3 x 68.6 cm)
Courtesy of Wright 20
R Producer: Droog/DMD
Various sizes (set of 3)
Courtesy of Droog
Photograph by Marsel Loermans

116

L Producer: Galerie Kreo
H 45 1/2", W 118 1/2", D 29 1/2" (115.6 x 301 x 74.9 cm)
Courtesy of Phillips de Pury & Company
R Producer: DMD/Droog
H 28 1/3", W 17 1/3", D 15" (71.9 x 43.9 x 38.1 cm)
Courtesy of Droog
Photograph by Gerard van Hees

117

L Producer: Edra
H 34 1/2", W 40", D 35" (87.6 x 101.6 x 88.9 cm)
Courtesy of Edra
R Producer: Design Gallery Milano
H 81", W 39 1/2", D 11 3/4" (205.7 x 100.3 x 29.8 cm)
Courtesy of Wright 20

118
L H 29", W 55 1/2", D 29" (73.7 x 141 x 73.7 cm)
Courtesy of Phillips de Pury & Company
R Producer: Mihoya Glass Co. Ltd.
H 34", W 35 1/2", D 24" (86.4 x 90.2 x 61 cm)
Courtesy of Phillips de Pury & Company

119
UL Producer: Källemo
H 34 1/4", W 19 1/4", D 20 3/4" (87 x 49 x 53 cm)
Courtesy of Källemo
LL Producer: Ishimaru Co., Ltd.
H 21", W 25", D 24" (53.3 x 63.5 x 61 cm)
Courtesy of Wright 20
UR Producer: Brickel Associates
H 15 1/4", W 16", D 16" (39 x 41 x 41 cm)
Courtesy of Wright 20
LR Producer: Knoll International
H 14 1/2", W 48", D 48" (36.8 x 121.9 x 121.9 cm)
Courtesy of Wright 20

120
L Producer: Wood and Plywood Furniture
H 45 3/4", W 80 1/2", D 44" (116.1 x 204.5 x 111.8 cm)
Courtesy of Phillips de Pury & Company
R **Courtesy of Swedese**

121
L H 41 3/4", W 15", D 15 3/4" (106 x 38.1 x 40 cm)
Courtesy of Phillips de Pury & Company
R Producer: DMD/Droog
H 32 1/3", W 32 1/3", D 30" (82 x 82 x 76.2 cm)
Courtesy of Droog

123
U Producer: PP Mobler
H 38 1/4", W 44", D 37" (97 x 112 x 94 cm)
Courtesy of PP Mobler
L Producer: Louis Poulsen
H 28", DIA 19" (71.1, 48.3 dia cm)
Courtesy of Wright 20

124
UL Producer: Cappellini
H 43", W 36", D 34" (109.2 x 91.4 x 86.4 cm)
Courtesy of Rago Arts and Auction Center
UR H 28 1/4", W 28 3/4", D 36" (71.8 x 73 x 91.4 cm)
Courtesy of Wright 20
LL H 32", W 78", D 18 1/5" (81.3 x 198.1 x 46.2 cm)
Courtesy of Rago Arts and Auction Center
LR Producer: Asko
H 48", W 47 1/4", D 40" (121.9 x 120 x 101.6 cm)
Courtesy of Wright 20

125
Producer: Harvey Probber, Inc.
H 27 1/2", W 90", D 29" (69.9 x 228.6 x 73.7 cm)
Courtesy of Wright 20

126
L Producer: Erik Jørgensen
H 25 1/4", W 78 3/4", D 60" (64 x 200 x 147 cm)
Courtesy of Erik Jørgensen
R Producer: Louise Campbell
H 29 1/2", W 33 1/2", D 39 1/2" (75 x 85 x 100 cm)
Courtesy of Louise Campbell Studio
Photograph by Brahl Fotografi

127
U Producer: Iform
H 28", W 30 3/4", D 24" (74 x 45 x 59 cm)
Courtesy of Iform
LL Producer: Edra
H 30 1/2", W 34", D 25" (77.5 x 86.4 x 63.5 cm)
Courtesy of Edra
LC Producer: Arteluce
H 16", W 13", D 13" (40.6 x 33 x 33 cm)
Courtesy of Rago Arts and Auction Center
LR Producer: Atelier Grunert
H 15 1/2", W 15 1/2", D 15 1/2" (40 x 40 x 40 cm)
Courtesy of Rago Arts and Auction Center

128
U Producer: Campana Objetos Ltda.
H 31 1/2", W 64", D 30 1/2" (80 x 162.6 x 77.5 cm)
Courtesy of Phillips de Pury & Company
L Producer: Bengtsson Design Ltd
H 31 1/2", W 21 1/2", D 21" (80 x 55 x 53 cm)
Courtesy of Bengtsson Design Ltd.
Photograph by Êjeppe Gudmundsen Holmgreen

130
U Producer: Moroso
(Pictured combination) H 39", W 102 7/8", D 35" (99.1 x 261.3 x 88.9 cm)
Courtesy of Moroso
L Producer: Cappellini
H 28 3/4", W 98 1/2", D 39 1/4" (73 x 250.2 x 99.7 cm)
Courtesy of Cappellini

131
U Producer: Vitra
Single component: H 12 1/2", W 10" (31.8 x 25.4 cm); 25 components make up a screen of H 36", W 36" (91.4 x 91.4 cm)
Courtesy of Vitra
Photograph by Andreas Sütterlin
L Producer: Magis
H 13 7/8", W 22", D 10 1/4" (35.1 x 55.9 x 25.9 cm)
Courtesy of Magis

132
U Producer: Solidity Ltd.
H 57 1/2", W 52 3/5", D 15 3/4" (146 x 133.6 x 40 cm)
Courtesy of Wolfson Design
Photograph by Maxin Nilov
L Producer: Artecnica, Inc.
Courtesy of Artecnica, Inc.

133
L Producer: Christophe Come
H 68 7/8", W 36 1/4", D 18 7/8" (175 x 92 x 48 cm)
Courtesy of Cristina Grajales Inc.
UR Producer: Källemo
Chair: H 30", W 17 4/5", D 15 2/5" (76.3 x 45.2 x 39 cm); Desk: H 16 1/3", W 17 4/5", D 17 4/5" (41.3 x 45.2 x 45.2 cm)
Courtesy of Komplot
LR Producer: Galerie Kreo
H 29 1/8", W 70 7/8", D 35 1/2" (73.9 x 179.8 x 90.2 cm)
Courtesy of Galerie Kreo
© Fabrice Gousset

134
L Producer: Dahlström
Courtesy of Dahlström Design AB

R Producer: Magis
H 30 3/4", W 40", D 25 1/4" (78 x 101.6 x 64 cm)
Courtesy of Magis

135
U Producer: Swedese
(1 piece, 5 pieces pictured) H 16 1/8", W 16 1/8", D 16 1/8" (40.9 x 40.9 x 40.9 cm)
Courtesy of Swedese
L Producer: Galerie Kreo
H 15 3/4", W 64 1/8", D 36 5/8" (40 x 162.8 x 93 cm)
Courtesy of Galerie Kreo
©Fabrice Gousset

136
UL Producer: Magis
Table (rectangle top): H 28 3/4", 37 2/5", W 55 1/8", D 35 2/5" (73, 95 x 140 x 90 cm)
Courtesy of Magis
LL Producer: Klaessons
H 33", W 80", D 27 3/4" (79 x 44 x 74 cm)
Courtesy of Klaessons
UR Producer: Chris Rucker
H 31 3/4", W 29", D 17 1/2" (80.6 x 73.7 x 44.5 cm)
Courtesy of Industry Gallery
LR Producer: Handmade by Tom Dixon
H 32 1/2" (82.6 cm)
Courtesy of Phillips de Pury & Company

137
L Producer: Kartell, Habitat Division
H 32 3/4", W 21 1/3", D 21 1/3" (83 x 54 x 54 cm)
Courtesy of Kartell, Habitat Division
UR Producer: Raphaël Charles
Variable Thickness, DIA 74 4/5" (190 cm)
Courtesy of NextLevel Galerie
Photograph by Raphaël Charles
LR H 23", W 57", D 27" (58.4 x 144.8 x 144.8 cm)
Courtesy of Paul Kasmin Gallery
Photograph by Christopher Burke

138
Producer: b.d Barcelona Design
H 66", W 35 1/2", D 32" (167.6 x 90.2 x 81.3 cm)
Courtesy of Hayon Studio

139
U Producer: Marc Newson
H 39 3/4", W 97 1/4", D 28 1/4" (101 x 247 x 71.8 cm)
Courtesy of Phillips de Pury & Company
L Producer: Vladimir Kagan
Courtesy of Rago Arts and Auction Center

140
L Producer: Cappellini
H 28 1/4", W 78 3/4", D 39 1/4" (71.8 x 200 x 99.7 cm)
Courtesy of Cappellini
R Producer: Klaus Nienkämper
H 35 1/2", W 46 1/2" (90.2 x 118.1 cm)
Courtesy of Phillips de Pury & Company

141
L Producer: Artek
(As pictured) H 33 1/8", W 15 3/4", D 17 1/3" (84 x 40x 44 cm)
Courtesy of Artek
R Producer: Philip Michael Wolfson
H 24 4/5", W 24 1/2", D 27 5/8" (63 x 62.2 x 70.1 cm)
Courtesy of Phillips de Pury & Company

142
UL Producer: Ralph Pucci International
H 43", W 120", D 36" (17 x 305 x 14.2 cm)
Courtesy of Ralph Pucci International
Photograph by Antoine Bootz
UR Bronze elements sand-cast by H. Theophile
H 13 1/2", W 44 1/2", D 44 1/2" (34.3 x 113 x 113 cm)
Courtesy of Phillips de Pury & Company
L Producer: Established & Sons
H 28 1/3"-29 7/8", W 120", D" 53 1/8" (71.9-75.9 x 304.8 x 134.9 cm)
Courtesy of Established & Sons
Photograph by Peter Guenzel

143
U Producer: Cappellini
H 14 1/2", 25 1/2", W 94 1/2", D 63" (36.8, 64.8 x 240 x 160 cm)
Courtesy of Cappellini
L Producer: B & B Italia
H 33 7/8", W 88 5/8", D 37 3/8" (86 x 225 x 95 cm)
Courtesy of B & B Italia

144
L H 30 1/2", W 65", D 25 1/2" (77.5 x 165.1 x 64.8 cm)
Courtesy of Wright 20
R Producer: Wästberg
H 19 3/4", W 4 3/4", D 15 2/5" (50 x 11 x 39 cm)
Courtesy of Claesson Koivisto Rune

145
U Producer: Vitra
H 30 1/2", W 115 1/4", D 39 1/2" (77.5 x 292.7 x 100.3 cm)
Courtesy of Vitra
LL Producer: Galerie Kreo
H 74 7/8", W 55 1/8", D 26 7/8" (190 x 140 x 68.1 cm)
Courtesy of Galerie Kreo
© Fabrice Gousset
LR Producer: Moroso
H 30", W 20 1/2", D 20" (76 x 52 x 51 cm)
Courtesy of Moroso

146
L Producer: Joris Laarman Studio
H 29 1/2", W 149 1/2", D 47 1/4" (74.9 x 379.7 x 119.9 cm)
Courtesy of Friedman Benda
R Producer: Kartell, Habitat Division
H 37", W 21 1/3", D 21 3/4" (94 x 54.1 x 55.1 cm)
Courtesy of Kartell, Habitat Division

147
U Producer: Philippe Malouin Studio
H 39 1/2", DIA 9 7/8" (100.3 x 24.9 dia cm)
Courtesy of NextLevel Galerie
© Rene van der Hulst
L Producer: Galerie Kreo
H 25", W 78", D 19 5/8" (63.5 x 198.1 x 49.8 cm)
Courtesy of Galerie Kreo
©Fabrice Gousset

148
UL Producer: Klaessons
Courtesy of Klaessons
LL Producer: Toolsgalerie
H 12 1/5", W 41 1/3", D 55 1/8" (31 x 104.9 x 140 cm)
Courtesy of Toolsgalerie
UR Producer: Treluce
H 24", W 36", D 5" (61 x 91.4 x 12.7 cm)
Courtesy of Treluce Studios

CR Producer: Offecct
H 28 3/4", W 66", D 26" (73 x 168 x 66 cm)
Courtesy of Offecct
Photograph by Peter Fotograf
LR Producer: Aranda\Lasch for Johnson Trading Gallery
H 30" W 72", D 18" (76.2 x 45.7 x 182.9 cm)
Courtesy of Phillips de Pury & Company

149
U Producer: Eilersen
H 23 1/4", W 118", D 71" (59 x 300 x 180 cm)
Courtesy of Eilersen
L Producer: Form Verk
H 13 3/4", W 94 1/2", D 47 1/4" (35 x 240 x 120 cm)
Courtesy of From Verk

150
L Producer: Galerie Italienne
H 22", W 85", D 58 1/4" (55.9 x 215.9 x 148 cm)
Courtesy of Phillips de Pury & Company
R Producer: Moooi
H 93 3/4", W 62 1/5", D 26 4/5" (238 x 158 x 68 cm)
Courtesy of Moooi

151
UL Producer: Frank Willems
H 22 2/5", W 25 3/5", D 25 3/5" (56.9 x 65 x 65 cm)
Courtesy of Frank Willems
UR Producer: Magis
(pictured combination) H 24 1/2", W 52 1/4", D 12 1/4" (62.2 x 132.6 x 31 cm)
Courtesy of Magis
L Producer: Vivero
Single Unit: H 31", W 22", D 23 3/4" (79 x 56 x 73 cm)
Courtesy of Vivero

152
UL Producer: Dune
H 63", W 206 3/4", D 175 1/4" (160 x 525 x 445 cm)
Courtesy of Claesson Koivisto Rune
LL Producer: NextLevel Galerie
Chair: H 30 3/4", W 33 1/8", D 25 3/5" (78 x 84.1 x 65 cm); Ottoman: H 22 2/5", W 22 3/5", D 16 7/8" (56.9 x 57.4 x 42.9 cm)
Courtesy of NextLevel Galerie
Photograph by Charly Leborgne
UR Producer: Fredericia
H 31 1/2", W 47 1/4", D 39 2/5" (80 x 120 x 100 cm)
Courtesy of Fredericia
CR Producer: Lehrecke
Coffee table: H 16", W 46", D 33" (41 x 117 x 84 cm); Lamp-Side table: H 48", W 21", D 24" (122 x 54 x 61 cm)
Courtesy of Ralph Pucci International
Photograph by Antoine Bootz
LR Producer: Offecct
3 tables pictured: H 11 1/2", W 28 1/3", D 32 3/4" (29 x 72 x 83 cm); H 12 1/2", W 47 1/4", D 32 3/4" (32 x 120 x 83 cm); H 13 3/4", W 47 1/4", D 43 1/3" (35 x 120 x 110 cm)
Courtesy of Offecct

153
Producer: Offecct
Sofa: H 38 1/4", W 99 1/4", D 49 1/4" (97 x 252 x 125 cm); Ottoman: H 17 1/3", W 42 1/2", D 23 1/4" (44 x 108 x 59 cm)
Courtesy of Offecct

154
U Producer: Studio Job
H 79", W 134" (as shown), D 18" (200 x 340.4 x 45.7 cm)
Courtesy of Moss
L Producer: Bernhardt Design
10 modules in sizes from H 19 1/4"-25 1/3", W 29 1/2"-64 1/4", D 35 1/4"-47 1/4" (48.9-64.3 x 74.9-163.2 x 89.5-120 cm)
Courtesy of Bernhardt Design

155
L Producer: Moooi
H 26 3/4", W 34 1/3", D 28 3/4" (68 x 87 x 73 cm)
Courtesy of Moooi
R Producer: Mouvements Modernes
H 20 7/8", W 41 3/4", D 12 5/8" (53.1 x 106 x 32 cm)
Courtesy of Phillips de Pury & Company

156
U Producer: Galerie Kreo
Metallic tube: H 72 7/8", W 21 7/8", D 24 7/8" (184.9 x 55.4 x 63 cm); lampshade: H 15", DIA 51 1/4" (38.1 x 130.2 dia cm)
Courtesy of Galerie Kreo
© Fabrice Gousset
L Producer: Front Design
Courtesy of Front Design

157
U Producer: Cassina
Courtesy of Cassina
C Producer: Moroso
H 30", W 81 1/2", D 36 1/4" (76.2 x 207 x 92.1 cm)
Courtesy of Moroso
L Producer: Studio Job
H 30", W 39" (76.2 x 99 x 47.6 cm)
Courtesy of Moss

158
UL H 40", W 17", D 80" (101.6 x 43.2 x 203.2 cm)
Courtesy of Friedman Benda
LL Producer: Galerie Kreo
H 36 1/2", W 86", D 44 1/2" (92.7 x 218.4 x 113 cm)
Courtesy of Galerie Kreo
© Fabrice Gousset
UR Producer: Bernhardt Design
Courtesy of Bernhardt Design
LR Producer: Offecct
H 28 1/3", W 28", D 28 1/3" (72 x 71 x 72 cm)
Courtesy of Offecct

159
U Producer: Karl Schroth for ARPA Industriale S.p.A.
H 84 3/4", W 39 3/8", D 74 4/5" (215 x 190 x 100 cm)
Courtesy of PeLiDesign
Photograph by Kees Martens
L Producer: Vitra
Varying widths, H 53 1/2", D 33" (135.9 x 83.8 cm)
Courtesy of Vitra
Photograph by Marc Eggimann

160
Producer: Meritalia
H 43 1/3", W 111", D 37" (110 x 282 x 94 cm)
Courtesy of Meritalia

161
L Producer: Droog/DMD
H 81", W 33", D 45" (205.7 x 83.8 x 114.3 cm)
Courtesy of Phillips de Pury & Company
R Producer: Carpenters Workshop Gallery
H 41 1/3", W 55 1/8", D 33 1/2" (105 x 140 x 85 cm)
Courtesy of Carpenters Workshop Gallery

162
UL Producer: Godspeed
H 39 1/2", W 19 3/4", D 19 3/4" (100 x 50 x 50 cm)
Courtesy of Godspeed
UR Producer: Galerie Kreo
H 46 1/2", DIA 15 5/8" (118.1 x 39.6 dia cm)
Courtesy of Galerie Kreo
©Fabrice Gousset
L Producer: Established & Sons
(8 Drawers Pictured) H 42 1/2", W 22 1/5", D 24 1/5" (108 x 56.5 x 61.5 cm)
Courtesy of Established & Sons

163
L Producer: Harush Shlomo
H 56", W 32", D 24" (142 x 81 x 61 cm)
Courtesy of Industry Gallery
UR Producer: Galerie Kreo
H 79 ", W 110 1/2", D 41 1/4" (201 x 281 x 105.5 cm)
Courtesy of Galerie Kreo
© Paul Tahon + R. & E. Bouroullec
LR Producer: Carpenters Workshop Gallery
H 64 1/8", W 63 3/4", D 15 1/3" (163 x 162 x 39 cm)
Courtesy of Carpenters Workshop Gallery

164
L Producer: Mathias Bengtsson
H 30" (76.2 cm)
Courtesy of Phillips de Pury & Company
R Producer: Bernhardt Design
H 30 1/2", W 23", D 27" (77.5 x 58.4 x 68.6 cm)
Courtesy of Bernhardt Design

165
U Producer: Affina Marine Ltd
H 29 1/8", W 94 1/2", D 35 2/5" (74 x 240 x 90 cm)
Courtesy of Wolfson Design
C Producer: Established & Sons
H 16 1/2", W 113 1/2", D 34 1/2" (41.9 x 288.3 x 87.6 cm)
Courtesy of Established & Sons
Photograph by Peter Guenzel
L Producer: Cappellini
Single unit (three units pictured): H 41 1/4", W 73 3/4", D 15 3/4" (104.8 x 187.3 x 40 cm)
Courtesy of Cappellini

166
UL Producer: Friedman Benda, in conjunction with Front Design
H 30 1/4" (76.8 cm)
Courtesy of Phillips de Pury & Company
LL Producer: Moroso
Courtesy of Moroso
UR Producer: Joris Laarman Studio
H 29 7/8", W 17 3/4", D 30 1/3" (75.7 x 45 x 77 cm)
Courtesy of Friedman Benda

LR Producer: Plank
H 31 7/8", W 18 1/2", D 15 3/4" (81 x 47 x 39.9 cm)
Courtesy of Plank

167
UL Producer: .MGX by Materialise
H 31" (78.7 cm)
Courtesy of Phillips de Pury & Company
UR Producer: .MGX by Materialise
H 31", W 21", D 16" (78.5 x 53.8 x 40.5 cm)
Courtesy of .MGX by Materialise
L Producer: Demakersvan
H 32", W 52", D 40" (81.3 x 132.1 x 101.6 cm)
Courtesy of Carpenters Workshop Gallery

168
Producer: Established & Sons
(Low Cabinet Pictured) H 25 2/5", W 102 2/5", D 15 7/8" (64.5 x 260 x 40.5 cm)
Courtesy of Established & Sons

169
UL Hanging Platform: W 60", D 60" (152.4 x 152.4 cm); Lamp: DROP 82 3/4", DIA 59 1/8" (210.1 x 150.1 cm)
UR Producer: Moooi
H 31 7/8", W 26 2/5", D 48 2/5" (81 x 67.1 x 122.9 cm)
Courtesy of Moooi
Courtesy of Haunch of Venison
LL Producer: Reestore
H 29 1/2", W 29 1/2", D 35 2/5" (74.9 x 74.9 x 89.9 cm)
Courtesy of Reestore
LR Producer: Established & Sons
H 25 3/5", W 27 1/5", D 26" (65 x 69 x 66 cm)
Courtesy of Established & Sons

170
UL H 36 1/4", W 25 1/4", D 21 3/4" (92 x 64 x 55 cm)
Courtesy of Nilufar
LL Producer: HAY
H 30 3/4", W 23 1/3", D 28 1/8" (78 x 59.2 x 71.3 cm)
Courtesy of Komplot
UR Producer: Källemo
H 33 1/2", W 18 1/2", D 19 1/3" (85 x 47 x 49 cm)
Courtesy of Källemo
LR Producer: NextLevel Galerie
H 17 3/4", W 15 3/4", D 90 3/5" (45 x 39.9 x 230.1 cm)
Courtesy of NextLevel Galerie
© Nick Ballon

171
L Producer: Rolu Studios
H 33.75", W 25.5", D 35
Courtesy of Rolu Studios
R Producer: HIVE
Courtesy of HIVE

172
Producer: Moroso
H 32 3/4", W 30 1/3", D 32 3/4" (83.2 x 77 x 83.2 cm)
Courtesy of Moroso

173
U Producer: René Veenhuizen and Tejo Remy
H 96", W 136", D 87" (244 x 345 x 221 cm)
Courtesy of Industry Gallery
L H 45", D 60" (114.3 x 152.4 cm)
Courtesy of R 20th Century Design
Photograph by Sherry Griffin

174
U Producer: Nigel Coates
H 18", W 34 1/2", D 47" (46 x 88 x 94 cm)
Courtesy of Cristina Grajales Inc.

L H 31 1/3", W 61 4/5", D 24" (79.5 x 157 x 61 cm)
Courtesy of Paul Kasmin Gallery

175
L H 23 3/5", W 29 7/8", D 41 1/3" (59.9 x 75.9 x 104.9 cm)
Courtesy of Toolsgalerie
L Producer: Maison Gerard Ltd.
H 16", DIA 13", DROP 27" (40.6 x 33 dia x 68.6 drop cm)
Courtesy of Maison Gerard Ltd.

176
Producer: Ron Arad Associates
H 35 1/2", W 86", D 38" (90.2 x 218.4 x 96.5 cm)
Courtesy of Phillips de Pury & Company

177
UL Producer: Sebastian Errazuri
H 63 7/8", W 33", D 33" (162.1 x 83.8 x 83.8 cm)
Courtesy of Galerie Kreo
©Fabrice Gousset
UR Producer: Estudio Campana
H 37 1/2", W 19 1/2", D 23 1/2" (95.3 x 49.5 x 59.7 cm)
Courtesy of Phillips de Pury & Company
L Producer: Cristophe Come
H 26 3/4", W 63", D 20" (70 x 160 x 51 cm)
Courtesy of Cristina Grajales Inc.

178
Producer: Hugo Franca
H 33", W 74 3/4", D 65 3/4" (83.8 x 189.9 x 167 cm)
Courtesy of R 20th Century Design

179
L Producer: Walz
H 32 1/4", W 20 1/2", D 17 1/4" (82 x 52 x 44 cm)
Courtesy of Ralph Pucci International
Photograph by Antoine Bootz
R H 28 1/2", W 21 1/2", D 19 1/2" (72.4 x 54.6 x 49.5 cm)
Courtesy of Moderne Gallery
Photograph by Gil Amiaga

180
UL Producer: Bristow-Proffitt
Bookhaus: H 92", W 100", D 15" (234 x 254 x 38 cm); Jack Chair: H 38 1/2", W 13", D 38" (98 x 33 x 96.5 cm)
Courtesy of Ralph Pucci International
Photograph by Antoine Bootz
UR Producer: Handmade by Max Lamb
H 28 1/2" (72.4 cm)
Courtesy of Phillips de Pury & Company
LR Producer: Droog/DMD
H 29 1/2", W 102 2/5", D 35 2/5" (75 x 260 x 90 cm)
Courtesy of Droog

181
UL Desk: H 33", W 66", D 39" (83.8 x 167.6 x 99.1 cm); Chair: H 43 1/2", W 24 3/4", D 24" (110.5 x 62.9 x 61 cm)
Courtesy of Wright 20

UR Producer: Nilufar
H 36 1/2", W 27 1/4", D 22 1/2" (93 x 69 x 57 cm)
Courtesy of Nilufar
L Producer: Toolsgalerie
H 39 2/5", W 19 3/4", D 11 4/5" (100.1 x 50.2 x 30 cm)
Courtesy of Toolsgalerie

182
L Producer: Brühl
H 34 5/8", W 90 5/8", D 49 5/8" (87.9 x 230.1 x 126 cm)
Courtesy of Brühl
UR Producer: Moroso
H 30 1/3", W 23 1/2", D 22 3/4" (77 x 60 x 58 cm)
Courtesy of Moroso
LR Producer: QisDesign
(Each crystal) DIA 2 7/8" (7.3 cm)
Courtesy of QisDesign

183
UL Producer: Nendo
H 30", W 28", D 26" (76.2 x 71.1 x 66 cm)
Courtesy of Friedman Benda
UR Producer: Droog/DMD
H 29 1/2", W 39 1/2", D 27 5/8" (74.9 x 100.3 x 70.1 cm)
Courtesy of Droog
Photograph by Gerard van Hees
L **Courtesy of Priveekollektie**

184
Producer: Nilufar
H 23 1/4", W 78", D 28" (59 x 198 x 71 cm)
Courtesy of Nilufar

185
L H 27 1/2", W 37 1/2", D 37 1/2" (70 x 95.3 x 95.3 cm)
Courtesy of Industry Gallery
R Producer: Cappellini
H 30 1/4", W 21 1/4", D 17 1/4" (76.8 x 54 x 43.8 cm)
Courtesy of Cappellini

186
L Drop 94 1/2" (240 cm)
Courtesy of Phillips de Pury & Company
187 [?]

C Producer: Ingo Maurer GmbH
H 39 3/8", DIA 27 1/2" (100 x 69.9 dia cm)
Courtesy of Ingo Maurer GmbH
R Producer: Godspeed
H 23 1/2", Radius 23 1/2" (60 x 60 cm)
Courtesy of Godspeed

187
UL DROP 78 3/4", DIA 59" (200 x 150 dia cm)
Courtesy of Phillips de Pury & Company
UR Producer: Moroso
H 32 3/4", W 28", D 24 3/4" (83 x 71 x 63 cm)
Courtesy of Moroso
L Producer: Nilufar
Courtesy of Priveekollektie

188
UL Producer: EJ Jorgensen
H 26 3/4", W 95 1/4" (68 x 243 cm)
Courtesy of EJ Jorgensen
UR Producer: Swarovski
57 x 65 x 35 (cm? inches?)
Courtesy of Phillips de Pury & Company
L Producer: Magis
Dog House: H 29 3/4", W 19 1/8", D 35" (75.4 x 48.5 x 88.9 cm); Steps: H 6 3/4", W 12", D 10 1/2" (17 x 30.5 x 26.7 cm)
Courtesy of Magis

189
L Producer: Estudio Campana
H 61", W 37 1/2", D 43 1/3" (154.9 x 95.3 x 110 cm)
Courtesy of Phillips de Pury & Company
R H 80 1/2", W 35", D 28" (204.5 x 88.9 x 71.1 cm)
Courtesy of Paul Kasmin Gallery

190
UL Producer: Albion Gallery
H 31 1/2", W 15 3/4", D 21 3/4" (80 x 39.9 x 55.1 cm)
Courtesy of Phillips de Pury & Company
LL Producer: Eiji Shibata
H 34", W 19 1/2", D 26 3/4" (86 x 50 x 68 cm)
Courtesy of Coolhouse Antiques
UC Producer: Plank
H 32 1/3", W 20 1/8", D 21 3/4" (82 x 51.1 x 55.1 cm)
Courtesy of Plank
LC Producer: Magis
H 30 1/3", W 16 1/2", D 19 1/3" (77 x 42 x 49 cm)
Courtesy of Magis
UR Producer: Swedese
H 32 3/4", W 35", D 28" (83.1 x 88.9 x 71.1 cm)
Courtesy of Swedese
LR H 17 1/2", W 67 4/5", D 67 4/5" (44.5 x 171.8 x 124.5 cm)
Courtesy of Barry Friedman Ltd.
Photograph by Annsophie Lombrail

191
L Producer: .MGX by Materialise
H 15 3/4", Radius 12 1/2" (folded out) (40 x 32 cm)
Courtesy of .MGX by Materialise
R Producer: Lammhults
H 31 1/8", W 24 1/8", D 27 1/4" (81 x 63 x 69.2 cm)
Courtesy of Lammhults

192
Producer: Flindt Design
Each chair: H 34 5/8", W 22", D 16 5/8" (88 x 56 x 42 cm)
Courtesy of Flindt Design
Photograph by Magnus Klitten

Albera, Giovanni, and Nicolas Monti. *Italian Modern: A Design Heritage.* New York: Rizzoli, 1989.

Antonelli, Paola. *Objects of Design from the Museum of Modern Art.* New York: The Museum of Modern Art, 2003.

Baker, Fiona, and Keith Baker. *20th Century Furniture.* London: Carlton Books, 2000.

Bayley, Stephen, Philippe Garner, and Deyan Sudjic. *Twentieth-Century Style & Design.* New York: Van Nostrand Reinhold, 1986.

Coles, Alex, ed. *DesignArt.* London: Tate Publishing, 2005.

Collins, Michael, and Andreas Papadakis. *Postmodern Design.* New York: Rizzoli, 1989.

Fairs, Marcus. *21st Century Design: New Design Icons from Mass Market to Avant-Garde.* London: Carlton Books, 2009.

Fiell, Charlotte, and Peter Fiell. *Design Now.* Cologne: Taschen, 2008.

———. *Modern Furniture Classics Since 1945.* Washington, D.C.: AIA Press, 1991.

Fischer, Volker, ed. *Design Now: Industry or Art?* Munich: Prestel, 1989.

German Design Council, *German Design Award 201,.* Munich: Gestalten, 2010.

Greenberg, Cara. *Mid-Century Modern: Furniture of the 1950s.* New York: Harmony Books, 1984.

Gura, Judith. *Sourcebook of Scandinavian Furniture: Designs for the 21st Century.* New York: W.W. Norton & Company, 2007.

Heisinger, Kathryn, and Felice Fischer. *Japanese Design: A Survey Since 1950.* New York: Harry N. Abrams, 1994.

Heisinger, Kathryn, and George Marcus, *Landmarks of Twentieth-Century Design.* New York: Abbeville Press, 1993.

Hillier, Bevis. *Art Deco of the 20s and 30s.* New York, Littlehampton, 1968.

———. *The World of Art Deco: An Exhibition Organized by The Minneapolis Institute of Arts, June-September, 1971.* New York: E. P. Dutton, 1971.

Jackson, Lesley. *The Sixties: Decade of Design Revolution,* New York: Phaidon, 1998.

Jencks, Charles. *What is Postmodernism?* London: Academy Editions, 1986.

Johnson, W. Stewart. *Modern Design in the Met Museum of Art, 1890-1990.* New York: Harry N. Abrams, 1990.

Kelsey, John. *The Meaning of Craft.* Ashville, N.C..Furniture Society, 2007.

Klanten, R., et al, *Once Upon a Chair: Design Beyond the Icon.* Berlin: Gestalten, 2009.

Kron, Joan, and Suzanne Slesin, *High-Tech: The Industrial Style and Source Book for the Home.* New York: Clarkson Potter, 1978.

Kupetz, A., et al, *Desire, The Shape of Things to Come.* Berlin: Gestalten, 2008.

Lauria, Jo, and Suzanne Baizerman. *California Design.* San Francisco: Chronicle Books, 2005.

Lauria, Jo, and Steven Fenton, *Craft in America: Celebrating Two centuries of Artists and Objects.* New York: Clarkson Potter, 2007.

Marcus, George. *Design in the Fifties: When Everyone Went Modern.* Munich: Prestel, 1998.

McDonough, Michael, and Michael Braungart, *Cradle to Cradle: Remaking the Way We Make Things.* New York: North Point Press, 2002.

Meyer, B., et al, *Furnish: Furniture and Interior Design for the 21st Century.* Berlin: Gestalten, 2007.

Pile, John. *Furniture: Modern+Postmodern,;Design+Technology.* New York: John Wiley & Sons, 1990.

Polster, Bernd. *German Design for Modern Living: The Classics.* Berlin: DuMont Buchverlag, 2010.

Pulos, Arthur. *The American Design Adventure*. Cambridge, Mass.: MIT Press, 1988.

Radice, Barbara.*Memphis: Research, Experiences, Results, Failures and Successes of New Design*. New York, Rizzoli, 1984.

Ramakers, Renny, and, Giis Bakker, *Droog Design: Spirit of the 90s*. Rotterdam, 010 Publishers, 1998.

Sadler, Simon. *Archigram: Architecture without Architecture*. Boston: MIT Press, 2005.

Sparke, Penny. *Design in Italy: 1870 to the Present*. New York: Abbeville, 1988.

——,. *Japanese Design,*. New York: The Museum of Modern Art, 2008.

Stone, Michael. *Contemporary American Woodworkers*. Layton, Utat: Peregrine Smith, 1986.

Sudjic, Deyan, ed. *Design in Britain*. London: Conran, 2009.

Tambini, Michael. *The Look of the Century*. New York: Dorling Kindersley, 1996.

Vegesack, Alexander. *100 Masterpieces from the Vitra Design Museum Collection*. Weil Am Rhein: Vitra Design Museum, 1995.

Venturi, Robert, *Complexity and Contradiction in Architectur.*. New York: The Museum of Modern Art, 1966.

Venturi, Robert, and Denise Scott Brown, *Learning from Las Vegas*. Cambridge, Mass.: MIT Press, 1972.

Williams, Gareth. *The Furniture Machine: Furniture Since 1990*. London: Victoria & Albert Museum Publications, 2006.

Wines, James. *De-Architectur*e. New York: Rizzoli, 1987.

DESIGN AFTER MODERNISM

EXHIBITION-RELATED PUBLICATIONS

Ambasz, Emilio, ed. *Italy: The New Domestic Landscape.* New York: The Museum of Modern Art, 1972.

Antonelli, Paola. *Design and the Elastic Mind.* New York: The Museum of Modern Art, 2009.

Bloemink, Barbara. *Design ≠ Art.* New York: Cooper-Hewitt National Design Museum, 2004.

Bloemink, Barbara, et al. *Design Life Now.* New York: Cooper-Hewitt National Design Museum, 2006.

Clark, Robert Judson, and Andrea Belloli. *Design in America: The Cranbrook Vision, 1925–1950.* New York: Detroit Institute of Arts/ Metropolitan Museum of Art/Harry N. Abrams, 1983.

Clark, Robert Judson, ed, *The Arts & Crafts Movement in America, 1876-1916.* Princeton, N.J.: Princeton University Press, 1972.

Cooke, Edward, Jr., *New American Furniture: The Second Generation of Studio Furniture Makers.* Boston: MFA Publications, 1989.

———. Gerald Ward, and Kelly L'Ecuyer. *The Maker's Hand: American Studio Furniture, 1940–1990.* Boston: MFA Publications, 2003.

Crowley, David. *Cold War Modern: Design, 1945–1970.* London: Victoria & Albert Museum Publications, 2008.

Eidelberg, Martin, Paul Johnson, and Kate Carmel. *Design 1935–1965: What Modern Was.* New York: Musée des Arts Décoratifs de Montreal/Harry N. Abrams, 1991.

Heisinger, Kathryn, and George Marcus. *Design Since 1945.* New York: Philadelphia Museum of Art/Rizzoli, 1983.

Hillier, Bevis. *The World of Art Deco.* Minneapolis Institute of Arts/ Dutton, 1971.

Johnson, Philip, and Mark Wigley. *Deconstructivist Architecture.* New York: The Museum of Modern Art, 1988.

Kaplan, Wendy. *Art That is Life: The Arts & Crafts Movement in America, 1875-1920.* New York: Museum of Fine Arts Boston/ Bulfinch, 1987.

Kardon, Janet. *Craft in the Machine Age, 1920-1945.* New York: American Craft Museum/Harry N. Abrams, 1995.

Lambert, Phyllis. *Mies in America.* New York: Harry N. Abrams, 2001.

Riley, Terence. *The Un-Private House.* New York: The Museum of Modern Art, 1999.

Miller, R. Craig, P. Sparke, and C. McDermott. *European Design Since 1985: Shaping the New Century.* New York: Denver Art Museum/ Indianapolis Art Museum/Merrell, 2008.

Miller, R. Craig, ed. *U.S. Design: 1975–2000.* Munich: Denver Art Museum/Prestel, 2002.

Phillips, Lisa, and David Hanks, eds. *High Styles: Twentieth-Century American Design.* New York: Whitney Museum of American Art/ Summit, 1985.

Rapoport, Brooke, and Kevin Stayton. *Vital Forms: American Art & Design in the Atomic Age, 1940–1960.* New York: Brooklyn Museum of Art/Harry N. Abrams, 2001.

Riley, Terence, and Barry Bergdoll, eds. *Mies in Berlin.* New York: The Museum of Modern Art, 2001.

Varnedoe, Kurt. *Vienna 1900: Art, Architecture & Design.* New York: The Museum of Modern Art, 1986.

Williams, Gareth. *Telling Tales: Fantasy and Fear in Contemporary Design.* London, Victoria & Albert Museum Publications, 2009.

Wilson, Richard Guy, Dianne Pilgrim, and Dickran Tashjian, *The Machine Age in America, 1918-1941.* New York: Brooklyn Museum of Art/Harry N. Abrams, 1986.

ARTECNICA, INC.
508 South San Vicente Blvd.
Los Angeles, CA 90048
United States
(323) 655-6551
http://www.artecnicainc.com/

ARTEK
Lemuntie 3-5 B
00510 Helsinki
Finland
+358 (0)9 6132 5277
http://www.artek.fi/

ARTIFORT
Van Leeuwenhoekweg 20
5482 TK Schijndel
The Netherlands
31 (0) 73 658 00 20
http://www.artifort.com/

BENGTSSON DESIGN LTD.
17-25 Cremer street
London E2 8HD
United Kingdom
+44 (0) 79 61 161 733
http://www.bengtssondesign.com

B & B ITALIA
Strada Provinciale 32
22060 Novedrate (CO)
Italy
39 (031) 795 111
http://www.bebitalia.it

BERNHARDT
1839 Morganton Blvd.
P.O. Box 740
Lenoir, NC 28645
United States
(828) 758-9811
http://bernhardtdesign.com/

BRÜHL
Alter Bad Stebener Weg 1
Bad Steben Calsgrun, 95138
Germany
49 (0) 9288/955-0
http://www.bruehl.com/en

STUDIO/ LOUISE CAMPBELL
Eckersbergsgade 39
DK - 2100 Copenhagen
Denmark
http://www.louisecampbell.com/

CAPPELLINI
Poltrona Frau Group, USA
145 Wooster Street
New York, NY 10012
United States
(212) 777-7592
http://www.cappellini.it/

CARPENTERS WORKSHOP GALLERY
3 Albemarle Street
London, W1S 4HE
United Kingdom
44 (0)203 051 59 39
http://london@carpentersworkshopgallery.com/

CASSINA
Poltrona Frau Group, USA
145 Wooster Street
New York, NY 10012
United States
(212) 777-7592
http://www.cassina.com/
Claesson Koivisto Rune
Östgötagatan 50
116 64 Stockholm
Sweden
46 (8) 644 58 63
http:/www.ckr.se/

COOLHOUSE ANTIQUES
211 West 19th Street
New York, NY 10011
(212) 254-4790
http://www.coolhouseantiques.com/

DAHLSTRÖM DESIGN AB
Repslagargatan 17B
118 46 Stockholm
Sweden
46 (8) 673 42 00
http://www.dahlstromdesign.se/

DE SEDE AG
Oberes Zelgli 2
CH-5313 Klingnau
Switzerland
41 (56) 268 01 11
http://www.desede.ch/en

DROOG B.V.
Staalstraat 7A
1011 JJ Amsterdam
Netherlands
t +31 (0)20 - 523 5050
info@droog.com

DROOG NEW YORK
611 Broadway
New York, NY 10012
United States
(212) 941-8350
http://www.droog.com/

EDRA
Via Livornese est 106
56035 Perignano (PI)
Italy
39 (0587) 61 6660
http://www.edra.com/

N. EILERSEN A/S
Fabriksvej 2
DK-5485 Skamby
Denmark
45 6485 1008
sales@eilersen.eu
http://www.eilersen.eu/

EMECO
805 Elm Avenue
Hanover, PA 17331
United States
http://www.emeco.net/

ESTABLISHED & SONS
5-7 Wenlock Road
London, N1 7SL
United Kingdom
44 (0)20 7608 0990
http://www.establishedandsons.com/

FLINDT DESIGN
Christian Flindt Slagterhusgade 7a
1715 Copenhagen V.
Denmark

+45 26709918
www.flindtdesign.dk/

FORMVERK OY
Annankatu 5
00120 Helsinki
Finland
358 (0)9 6129 55
http://www.formverk.com/

FREDERICIA FURNITURE
Treldevej 183
7000 Fredericia
Denmark
45 7592 3344
sales@fredericia.com
http://www.fredericia.com

BARRY FRIEDMAN LTD.
515 West 26th Street
New York, NY 10001
United States
(212) 239-8600
www.barryfriedmanltd.com/

FRIEDMAN BENDA
515 West 26th Street
New York, NY 10001
United States
(212) 239-8700
http://www.friedmanbenda.com/

FRONT DESIGN
Tegelviksgatan 20
116 41 Stockholm
Sweden
46 8 710 01 70
everyone@frontdesign.se
http://www.designfront.org/

CRISTINA GRAJALES GALLERY
10 Greene Street
New York, NY 10013
United States
1 (212) 219-9941
www.cristinagrajalesinc.com/

GODSPEED
Tel Aviv, Israel
972 (0) 54 59 68 059
http://www.weareonlyinitforthemoney.com/

HANSEN & SØRENSEN (OneCollection)
Vesterled-19
DK-6950
Ringkøbing
Denmark
45 702 771 01Eilers
info@onecollection.com
http://www.onecollection.com

HAUNCH OF VENISON
6 Burlington Gardens
London, W1S 3ET
United Kingdom
44(0)20 7495 5050
http://www.haunchofvenison.com/

HAYON STUDIO LTD.
59 Frith Street
London, W1D 3JJ
United Kingdom
http://www.hayonstudio.com/

HIVE
14th Street NW
Washington, DC 20009
United States
(888) 889-9005
http://www.designbyhive.com/

INDUSTRY GALLERY
1358 Florida Avenue, NE
Washington, DC 20002
(202) 399 1730
http://industrygallerydc.com/

ERIK JØRGENSEN MØBELFABRIK A/S
Industrivænget 1
DK – 5700 Svendborg
Denmark
45 62 21 53 00
info@erik-joergensen.com
http://www.erik-joergensen.com

AGENCE PATRICK JOUIN ID
8, Passage de la Bonne Graine
75011 Paris
France
33 (0)1 55 28 89 20
agence@patrickjouin.com
http://www.patrickjouin.com/

KÄLLEMO
Box 605
331 26 Värnamo
Sweden
46 (0) 370 150 00
www.kallemo.se/

KARTELL HABITAT DIVISION
39 Greene Street
New York, NY 10013
United States
(212) 966-6665
http://www.kartell.it/

PAUL KASMIN GALLERY
293 Tenth Avenue
New York, NY 10001
United States
(212) 563-4474
www.paulkasmingallery.com/

KOMPLOT
Amager Strandvej 50
Copenhagen, DK-2300
Denmark
45 (32) 96 32 55
http://www.komplot.dk/

GALERIE KREO
31, rue Dauphine
75006 Paris
France
33 (0)1 53 10 23 00
http://www.galeriekreo.com/

LAMMHULTS
Växjövägen 41, Box 26
SE-360 30 Lammhult
Sweden
46 (0) 472-269500
http://www.lammhults.se/

J. LOHMANN GALLERY
P.O. Box 437
New York, NY 10021
United States
(212) 734-1445
http://www.jlohmanngallery.com/

MAGIS
Z.I. Ponte Tezze
Via Triestina accesso E
30020 Torre di Mosto (VE)
Italy
39 (0421) 319600
http://www.magisdesign.com/

MAISON GERARD LTD.
53 East 10th Street

New York, NY 10003
United States
(212) 674-7611
www.maisongerard.com/

MATERIA (KLAESSONS AB)
P.O. Box 340
Bredkärrsgatan 7
573 24 Tranås
Sweden
46 140 38 56 00
info@materia.se
http://www.materia.se

INGO MAURER GMBH
Kaiserstrasse 47
80801 Munich
Germany
49 (89) 381 6060
http://www.ingo-maurer.com/

MEMPHIS S.R.L.
Via Olivetti 9, 20010 Pregnana
Milanese,
Milano, Italy
P. Iva 06196580150
Tel. (+39) 02 93290663
memphis@memphis-milano.it
http://www.memphis-milano.it

MERITALIA
via Como 76/78
22066 Mariano Comense (CO)
Italy
39 (031) 743100
http://www.meritalia.it/

.MGX BY MATERIALISE
Technologielaan 15
3001 Leuven
Belgium
32 (16) 39 66 11
www.mgxbymaterialise.com/

MODERNE GALLERY
111 North 3rd Street
Philadelphia, PA 19106
United States
(215) 923-8536
http://www.modernegallery.com/

MOOOI
Minervum 7003
4817 ZL Breda
P.O. Box 5703
4801 EC Breda
The Netherlands
0031 (0) 76 5784444
http://www.moooi.com/

MOROSO
Via Nazionale, 60
33010 Cavalicco, Udine
Italy
39 (0432) 577111
http://www.moroso.it/

MOSS
150 Greene Street
New York, NY 10012
(212) 204-7100
(866) 888-6677 toll free
store@mossonline.com/
http://www.mossonline.com

NEXTLEVEL GALERIE
4 rue Pastourelle
75003 Paris
France
33 (0)1 71 20 23 88
http://www.nextlevelgalerie.com/

PP MOBLER
Toftevej 30
DK - 3450 Allerød
Denmark
45 4817 2106
www.pp.dk/

NILUFAR
32 via della Spiga
20121 Milano
Italy
39 (02)780193
http://www.nilufar.com/

OFFECCT
Box 100
SE-543 21 Tibro
Sweden
46 (0) 504-415 00
www.offecct.se/

PELIDESIGN
Alexander Pelikan
Tarwelaan 56
5632 KG Eindhoven
The Netherlands
31 (0) 6 4140 3687
http://www.pelidesign.com/

PHILLIPS DE PURY & COMPANY
450 Park Avenue
New York, NY 10022
+1 212 940 1300
450 West 15th Street
New York, NY 10011
United States
(212) 940-1200
http://www.phillipsdepury.com

PIIROINEN
Tehdaskatu 28
24100 Salo
Finland
(358) 2 770 610
http://www.piiroinen.com/

PLANK
Via Nazionale 35
I-39040 Ora (BZ)
Italy
39 (0471) 803 500
http://www.plank.it/

PORRO
Via per Cantù, 35
22060 Montesolaro (CO)
Italy
(39) 031 783266
http://www.porro.com/ita/

PRIVEEKOLLEKTIE
Pelsestraat 15
5256 AT Heusden aan de Maas
The Netherlands
31 (0) 416 663234
http://www.priveekollektie.com/

RALPH PUCCI INTERNATIONAL
44 West 18th Street
New York, NY 10011
United States
(212) 633-0452
http://www.ralphpucci.net/

Q IS DESIGN
18 Jihu Road
Neihu
Taipei, 114
Taiwan
http://qisdesign.com/

QUITTENBAUM ART AUCTIONS
Theresienstrasse 60
D-80333 Munich
Germany
49 (89) 273702125
http://www.quittenbaum.de

R 20TH CENTURY DESIGN
82 Franklin Street
New York, NY 10013
United States
(212) 343-7979
http://www.r20thcentury.com/

RAGO ARTS AND AUCTION CENTER
333 North Main Street
Lambertville, NJ 08530
United States
(609) 397-9374
http://www.ragoarts.com/

REESTORE
18 Cottage Road
Sandy
Bedfordshire, SG19 1DE
United Kingdom
44 (0)7 810 716775
http://www.reestore.com/

ROLU STUDIO
Minneapolis, Minnesota
(612) 239-6264
info@ro-lu.com
http://www.ro-lu.com/

SEBASTIAN + BARQUET
544 West 24th Street
New York, NY 10011
United States
(212) 691-3215
http://www.sebastianbarquet.com/

SKITSCH
Via Monte di Pietà, 11
Milano (MM Montenapoleone)
Italy
(39) 02 36 633065
http://www.skitsch.it/

STOKKE
http://www.stokke.com/en
HÅG Export
Scandinavian Business Seating AS
Fridtjof Nansens vei 12
P.O. Box 5055 Majorstuen
NO-0301 Oslo, Norway
47 22 59 59 00
www.haginc.com

SWEDESE
Formvägen
PO Box 156
SE-567 23 Vaggeryd
Sweden
46 (0) 393 797 00
www.swedese.se/

TOOLSGALERIE
119, rue vieille du temple
75003 Paris
France
33 (0) 1 42 77 35 80
http://www.toolsgalerie.com/

TRELUCE STUDIOS
New York, NY
United States
www.treluce.com/

UMBRA LLC
1705 Broadway
Buffalo, NY 14212
United States
(716) 892-8852
http://www.umbra.com/

VARIÉR FURNITURE (HÅG)
Haahjem
6260 Skodje
Norway
47 70244352
info@varierfurniture.com
http://varierfurniture.com

VIGNELLI ASSOCIATES
130 East 67 Street
New York, NY 10021

(212) 737-0538
info@vignelli.com
http://www.vignelli.com/

VITRA
The Vitra Store
29 Ninth Avenue
New York, NY 10014
United States
(212) 463-5700
http://www.vitra.com/

WOLFSON DESIGN
24 Palace Court
Studio 11A
London, W2 4HU
United Kingdom
44 (0) 20 7229 3221
www.wolfsondesign.com/

STUDIO FRANK WILLEMS
Kanaalstraat 8
5611 CT Eindhoven
Netherlands
31 (0)6 2834 0598
frank@frankwillems.net
http://www.frankwillems.net

WRIGHT20
1440 W Hubbard
Chicago, IL 60642
United States
(312) 563-0020
http://www.wright20.com/

INDEX OF DESIGNERS

DESIGN AFTER MODERNISM